Kingdom
DREAMING

Unleashing Your God-Given
Purpose and Passion

By
Christopher W. Brooks

ZOË LIFE
PUBLISHING
WORDS TO LIVE BY

© 2009 Christopher Brooks

Published by:
Zoe Life Publishing
P.O. Box 871066
Canton, MI 48187 USA
www.zoelifepub.com

Author: Christopher Brooks
Cover Design: Fikre Prince
Editorial Team: Scott Nesbitt, Denise Crittendon and Nicole J. Johnson

First U.S. Edition 2009

Publisher's Cataloging-In-Publication Data

Brooks, Christopher

Kingdom Dreaming

Summary: In this book, Pastor Brooks calls on every Christian to actively search for that Dream, immersing him or herself in prayer, Scripture, and fellowship with other Dreamers to truly become not what the world wants, but what God has ordained.

10 Digit ISBN 1-934363-383 Perfect Bound Soft Cover
13 Digit ISBN ISBN 978-1-934363-38-6 Perfect Bound Soft Cover

1.   Christianity, Apologetics, Purpose, Plans, Destiny, Jesus

Library of Congress Control Number: 2009925756

For current information about releases by Christopher Brooks or other releases from Zoe Life Publishing, visit our web site: http://www.zoelifepub.com

Printed in the United States of America

V5 10 08 09

Acknowledgements

I would like to thank the following individuals without whom the Kingdom Dreaming project would not have been possible:

Evangel Ministries Family

Thank you first and foremost to Rev. George & Shirley Bogle for investing in me and entrusting me with an anointed, dynamic ministry! I am grateful for your wisdom and insight which have helped shape me as the shepherd of our church.

To Pastors Phil Carr and Aaron Richardson: you are not only my right and left hands, but you are my brothers who have encouraged me and challenged me to never remain "comfortable" but continue to "sharpen the saw" and never allow my thirst for the truth of the Word of God to be quenched. I would be remiss if I did not thank your awesome wives and my sisters, Renee' and Trina. Thank you for not only embracing Kingdom Dreaming in your own lives, but seeing the vision and running with it!

To the clergy, leaders & congregation of Evangel Ministries: thank you for being the best team and church that a pastor could ever hope for!!

I have been blessed with a Dream Team of executive assistants who have helped me to do more and be more than I ever could on my own. You have each made major contributions toward the completion of this book, whether through proofreading, scheduling of writing weeks, or help in maneuvering through the publishing process. To Sherrie Smith, Renee Glaze and Min. Ian Watts, thank you!

To be in covenant with a solid group of men who I have watched strengthen and build up one another through tremendous challenges and triumphs has been one of the great joys of my life. I would like to thank my discipleship group Fred, Flynn, Carlos, Blake, Vince, Tyrone, Ian and Aaron for your faithfulness and allowing me to impart to you, Kingdom Dreaming.

Thank you to all of the instructors, students and alumni of the Detroit Bible Institute! You have been a wonderful, enthusiastic, group to teach! You literally draw the Word out of me with your insatiable desire to grow in your knowledge and understanding of the Word of God. I'm always anxious and eager for each new term to begin and for the blessed privilege to teach and learn with you.

Equipped For Life Media Team

To all of my faithful listeners who have allowed me to share Kingdom Dreaming with you, thank you. To our Media Director, Fikre Prince, we have come a long way but this is just the beginning. Thank you for your faithfulness. I want to thank the team that makes it all happen behind the scenes, Tiffany, Justin, LaKeisha, Bettie, Paul and a host of EFL Media volunteers.

Thank you to my friends at Salem Communications Detroit: Chris, Brad and Steve for your continual ideas, encouragement and partnership with EFL and me personally. You have been great friends throughout this amazing journey.

My Family, Friends and Mentors

To Dr. John Jelenik, Dr. Gene Mayhew, Patrick Smith and my professors at Michigan Theological Seminary: thank you for giving me a solid theological foundation. To the Oxford University, Wycliffe Hall Staff, Ian Smith, Michael Ramsden, Amy Orr-Ewing, Dr. John Lennox, Dr. Alister McGrath, and the OCCA class of 2008: thank you for teaching and challenging me to engage the culture with God's truth and love. I now believe that we may one day see Brooks vs. Dawkins for real (lol)!

To my dear friends and co-laborers in the Gospel, Pastor Taurence & Eva Lauchie' and Grace for the Nations Church, Sam & Diane Kwesa, Pastor Tim & Cindy Dilena, Pastor David and Errica Washington, Pastor Dexter and Kim Hardy, Dr. Crawford Loritts, The late Rev. Eddie Edwards and Min. Mary Edwards, Pastor Bob & Evelyn Hoey,

Pastor Steven & Sara Sebyala, and Missionaries Bob & Rocio Sundburg. Thank you all for the encouragement, words of wisdom and love, and for seeing in me the call that God has placed upon my life.

Last and most importantly, I want to thank my mom and dad for being by my side every step of the way. You have been the best and words can't express how indebted I am to you. Thanks for teaching me how to be a man! To my Ethiopian mom: for being a constant source of encouragement. To my brothers and sisters: Lolita, Kinio, Annette, Jennifer, Ahmed, Fikre and Eugene, thanks for keeping me humble and grounded and reminding me that no matter how much I achieve or fail in life, I will always have my family in my corner. To my beautiful wife and children, Yodit, Chris and Zoe: You have taken me places I never thought I could go, and shown me a love deeper than I ever thought I would know. Thank you!

Kingdom
DREAMING

*Unleashing Your God-Given
Purpose and Passion*

By
Christopher W. Brooks

Contents

Dear Kingdom Dreamer,

When was the last time you dreamed? When was the last time you allowed yourself to envision a goal or aspiration that far exceeded your current limitations, challenges, and circumstances? When was the last time you petitioned the Lord to do something great with your life in order to bring Him glory? By virtue of you picking up this book, chances are there is a deep desire burning inside of you for God to do something awesome with your life. I believe this is true for every Christian. God has placed a dream on the inside of our hearts and spirits that He wants us to live out before we die or He returns.

Christians are not meant to live their lives in selfishness, fearfully hoarding up resources with no view towards eternity. Rather, Christians are to live with a selfless abandon, risking all for the glory of God. That's what this book is all about. My challenge to you is to consider what your life would be like if you boldly tested the limits of passionate Christian commitment. Imagine if today you decided to fully obey Christ and began doing the very thing He called you to do regardless of the consequences. Imagine how many lives you could impact if you dared to live out your God-given purpose. Imagine how you could change the world if you allowed God to birth into you His dream for your life.

For many of us, this is a foreign way of thinking. But in his book *The Normal Christian Life,* Watchman Nee highlights the fact that far too often what Jesus intended to be the way all Christians live is viewed as being too extreme or radical for the average churchgoer. But a careful examination of the life of Jesus and His earliest followers reveals that their lives were just that: radical! These were not men and women who simply went to church on Sunday, studied their Bibles occasionally, and volunteered their time when their busy schedules permitted. No, these were fanatical followers of Christ who were so convinced of His message that they allowed their lives to be driven by their great desire to serve Him. They loved Him and wanted to please Him with all their hearts. This love led to a powerful pursuit of His presence. Once in His presence, the Lord breathed His vision for redeeming the world into their hearts and empowered them with all they would need to bring Him glory. Equipped with their King's Dream, they set out by faith to do great exploits in His name. And what we read in the New Testament is just a short sampling, a highlight reel of sorts, of the awesome acts they did to change the course of human history forever. As hard as it may be to believe, this is how He wants you and me to live our lives!

Growing up, my life revolved around sports. I was an avid baseball and basketball player, and I spent many afternoons playing football with neighborhood friends, dirtying up school clothes I should have changed beforehand. I daydreamed about hitting the winning home run in the seventh game of the World Series, and I dreamed of nailing the game-winning basket as time ran out in an NBA playoff game. At night I often lay in bed looking at the posters on my wall of my favorite athletes, hoping that one day I would grow up to be just like them. I would think, "Wouldn't it be great to be in a hall of fame and be respected as one of the best of all time?"

As I got older and grew spiritually, I realized

that God had other plans for me besides baseball, basketball, and football, but I never stopped dreaming of being a hall of famer.

Only now, I was dreaming of being a different type of hall of famer.

You see, I have always wanted to do great things with my life. Becoming a Christian allowed me to direct my passions more perfectly toward Christ. Since the day I got saved, I have searched for heroes, men and women of such great faith that I could be proud to hang their posters on my bedroom wall and fantasize about one day growing up to be just like them. I found my heroes of faith in Scripture: men like Abraham, Moses, Paul, and Timothy. As a matter of fact, to my amazement I discovered that the Bible even has a hall of fame. Hebrews 11 records the names of those who are in the "Hall of Fame of Faith." This is my dream: I want to one day be listed among those who were willing to sacrifice everything for the goal of bringing Christ glory. Like King David, my prayer is that, one day, history will look back on my life and declare, "He served his generation well."

This is also my hope for your life.

God did not create you and me to be trapped in the life-draining cycle of mediocrity that far too many Christians have accepted as their reality. The sad fact is that if you are like most believers, you've never known the transforming experience of an international mission trip; you've probably never known the exhilaration of having God use you to lead someone to the point of totally surrendering his or her life to the Lordship of Christ; and you almost certainly have never known the joy of starting a ministry that shapes the lives of your generation for the cause of Christ. But these are just some of the awesome experiences that God wants all His children to know. However, far too many of us have allowed secular obligations, fears, and materialism to rob us of the abundant life Jesus died for us to live. There is much more to life than what you are currently experiencing, and it's time for you to live out your destiny.

In his book, *The Dreamgiver,* Bruce Wilkerson chronicles the story of a young man named Ordinary who embarks on a journey from the land of Average so that he can live in the city called Greatness. I think the vast majority of Christians are tired of being trapped in ordinary, passionless lives and are dreaming of breaking free from the "Land of Average" in order to live a fuller life in God's Kingdom. Simply put, I believe many Christians are ready to discover and fulfill their Kingdom Dream.

For the past 15 years, I have had the privilege of living out my Kingdom Dream, as pastor of a wonderful church; the president of a Bible Institute; the host of an international radio and television broadcast; and a missionary. I have tried my best to use all of my time, talent, and treasure in service to Jesus. I recognize that God's call and mission for my life is to help people discover, protect, and fulfill their Kingdom Dreams. My prayer is that over the course of the chapters of this book, I will be a coach and mentor in your life, enabling you to live out the extraordinary purpose for which God created you. My prayer is that by reading this book, your soul will become infected with the King's Dream, and that together we will start an epidemic of passionate Kingdom Dreamers throughout the Body of Christ.

Let the dream begin.

Yours in Christ,

Pastor Chris

1

What Is a Kingdom Dream?

I love etymology, which is the study of words and phrases. My love affair with words most likely began as a young boy in my father's basement library. My father was a history teacher in the Detroit Public School system for nearly 30 years. He also had a strong interest in law and even sat for the California Bar Exam at one point in his life. This all adds up to the fact that my father possessed a vast library. It was there, amid all of his books, journals, newspapers, and magazines, that I discovered the power of words.

Words, in my opinion, are the most powerful instruments given to mankind. I do not think that it is a coincidence that the Apostle John opens his Gospel by proclaiming:

In the beginning was the Word, and the Word was with God, and the Word was God **(John 1:1).**

In his book, *Time For Truth: Living Free in a World of Lies, Hype & Spin*, Os Guinness states that "one word of truth has more might than all the military with its weapons and artillery." Words shape the thoughts that eventually become the actions of mankind. That is why words and phrases should never be taken lightly. Words merit investigation and research in order to ensure proper understanding.

As a pastor, I am constantly attempting to communicate with diverse audiences, both domestically and internationally. I have found that one of the most embarrassing moments for a speaker—and frustrating experiences for a listener—occurs when a potentially great speech has failed to reach a person's heart or mind because of a lack of careful explanation of a particular word or phrase. As Christians, we are especially guilty of committing this oratory crime by using spiritual terms when engaging with unspiritual people. Very few non-Christians know what we mean when we ask questions such as "Are you saved?" or "Have you been born again?" These phrases, though common to us, demand definition if they are going to produce any fruitful dialogue.

Likewise, I realize that if this book is going to be beneficial, I must be very clear on what the phrase Kingdom Dream really means. How often have I found myself speaking on this topic with enthusiasm and fervor only to have a person stop me and kindly interrupt with the humbling question, "Sir, what is a Kingdom Dream?" With that in mind, let me provide you with a very basic definition of the term.

Simply put, a Kingdom Dream is the intersection at which God's plan for your life meets your passion to bring Him glory. Whenever these two forces collide, you have a bona fide Kingdom Dream.

Throughout this book I will unpack this term further, but for now let me explain how the concept of Kingdom Dreaming was born. About four years ago, I began to ponder a question that I am convinced the Lord placed in my heart. The question was a simple, yet radically profound, challenge to my thinking. One night, while preparing for a sermon, I found myself asking, "If I could do one great thing with my life in order to bring God glory before I die, what would it be?" I tried to shake it, but I was far too moved by the sheer wonder of the question and the purity of motives it seemed to produce within my heart. The more I considered the question, the more I found my focus shifting from my own wants and desires to His majesty and glory. From that day to the present, I cannot ponder that question without awakening something deep within me that drives me to want to celebrate His splendor and love with every action of my life.

On that night, when my mind presented my heart with a question that forced me to consider the true nature of my calling and purpose, it seemed as if my soul responded before my intellect could find the words to articulate what I felt so intensely. It was almost as if this was the question, the one question, my spirit had been longing for me to ask my entire life. The question would, in an amazing and unexpected way, unleash my life's calling to make the name of Jesus Christ famous throughout all the earth, especially to those of my generation.

I knew, that I could not forge ahead in my quest to answer that question and live out my response to it without having a strong theological foundation for my convictions. So, for months I searched the Scriptures diligently in hopes I had not been misled in my curiosity by the intrigue of a question that found no home in the Word of God. Much to my joy, it was not long before I was able to clearly see the Biblical underpinnings for the concept that would later become the message of my ministry. The following are just a few of the passages that spoke boldly to my mind:

For we are God's workmanship, created in Christ Jesus to do good works, which God prepared in advance for us to do (Ephesians 2:10).

In the same way, let your light shine before men, that they may see your good deeds and praise your Father in heaven (Matthew 5:16).

So whether you eat or drink or whatever you do, do it all for the glory of God (1 Corinthians 10:31).

"I have brought you glory on earth by completing the work you gave me to do" (John 17:4).

What these passages, and a litany of others, revealed was that God had predetermined a perfect plan for my life, and that the way to bring Him maximum glory would be to discover this plan and fulfill it. In some strange way my life became wonderfully simple. No longer was I overwhelmed by the myriad of options and opportunities that lay in front of me; nor was I aimlessly searching for some direction for my life. No, I had found a magnificent peace and joy in my life being unambiguously one-dimensional. I now had a single, exquisite goal, and that was to discover God's plan for my life and to abandon every other pursuit in my quest to bring Him glory.

I am just as convinced now as I was the day I fully embraced the ramifications of that life-changing realization that God has placed His purpose for our lives within our hearts. The sad truth is that it has taken countless hours in prayer, study of Scripture, and worship in His presence for His will to emerge to the forefront of my life. I believe this journey has been so arduous because over the course of my life I suppressed His glorious plan through my own carnal pursuits and ungodly religious activities. It was not easy to admit that much of what had been the foundation of my life had not come from Him and needed to be uprooted and replaced. I now realize that the quicker people can come to grips with the fact that they may have some deeply flawed and erroneous philosophies that need to be eradicated from their lives, the quicker they can begin the exciting journey to bring God glory.

For me, this expedition began with one transforming question I want you to seriously consider and allow to penetrate your heart: If you could do one great thing with your life in order to bring God glory before you die, what would it be? My passion and prayer is that this book will help you discover your own Kingdom Dream, and that you will spend the rest of your life living out the answer to that crucial question.

Kingdom Dream Devotional

Devotional Passage

Having then gifts differing according to the grace that is given to us, let us use them: if prophecy, let us prophesy in proportion to our faith; or ministry, let us use it in our ministering; he who teaches, in teaching; he who exhorts, in exhortation; he who gives, with liberality; he who leads, with diligence; he who shows mercy, with cheerfulness (Romans 12:6-8).

Kingdom Question

If you could do one great thing for God with your life, what would it be?

Dream Development Exercise

• Assessment Quiz @ www.teamministry.com.
• List your top three gifts.

2

Chosen by God

You may be familiar with the adage "let's start at the beginning," but when it comes to your Kingdom Dream, I believe it's best to start before the beginning. It is here, before the beginning, that God's awesome purpose was set in motion for your life. A proper study of Scripture reveals that God decided that He was going to use you to do great things for His Kingdom before you were even born.

We find a great example of this truth in the life of the prophet Jeremiah. The Book of Jeremiah chronicles the story of a man who, in many ways, is just like you and me. Jeremiah was called by God to do mighty things on His behalf. In spite of this, Jeremiah struggled with many fears and insecurities. He questioned whether God could use someone as ordinary and seemingly weak as he considered himself to be. In many ways, Jeremiah's purpose was in danger of ending before it even began. But God, as only He can, removed Jeremiah's fears simply by revealing to him the truth of His divine selection. Look at what God says in Jeremiah 1:5:

Before I formed you in the womb I knew you, before you were born I set you apart; I appointed you as a prophet to the nations.

The message that God wanted Jeremiah to know is that he need not wrestle with these questions of fear and doubt, because the Lord had already established an eternal purpose for his life. In essence, God was saying to Jeremiah, "Don't be afraid, insecure or fearful, but be confident, because I've chosen you." This is the message that He wants all of His children to know, understand, and believe: God has an eternal purpose for your life, and He wants you to be supremely confident in the path He has chosen for you.

Satan's greatest desire is that you will stop pursuing your purpose before you even get started. His hope is that you will convince yourself that somehow you are unable or ill-equipped to carry out God's plan, or that you are simply not called to greatness. Satan will do all he can to discourage you. He'll use tactics like encouraging you to meditate on previous failures, or bringing to your mind the negative words people have said about you. His hope is that you will disqualify yourself from ever attempting to do anything great with your life.

Sadly, many of us have taken Satan's bait. We have disqualified ourselves, even though God has called us. I want you to hear God's voice as it rises above that of your critics, your enemies, and your own insecurities. God declares, "I've chosen you to do great things on My behalf!"

There's a reason Satan is fighting against you embarking upon this journey to discovering and fulfilling your Kingdom Dream. The reason Satan is so afraid of you accomplishing your purpose is that, after spending considerable time contemplating your potential and God's plans for you, he realized the power a world full of Kingdom Dreamers would produce. Can you imagine his fear when he considers how many lives would be changed if you overcame your self-doubts and pursued your Kingdom Dream? He is overwhelmed with terror when he visualizes the impact you could have if you only believed what the Holy Spirit has to say about you.

This is why God has left His Word. He knows that, just like Jeremiah, you and I are going to need to be reminded that He hand-picked us to do something special on His behalf. Never forget that the Bible is the Kingdom Dreamer's best friend. His Word has the power to destroy every fear, worry, and doubt that Satan will send your way. The Bible also acts as your road map for discovering God's plan for your life, so cling tightly to His Word and remember what God told Joshua:

> *Do not let this Book of the Law depart from your mouth; meditate on it day and night, so that you may be careful to do everything written in it. Then you will be prosperous and successful* (Joshua 1:8).

Christians who don't know the Scriptures well will never fulfill the divine purpose for which they were created. Without a strong knowledge of the Word, they will be led by their emotions instead of by God's commandments and instructions. Many Christians have been deceived by Satan and tricked out of their purpose simply because they didn't seek God's Word or give it serious study and contemplation. By not actively seeking God, they miss the opportunity for their Kingdom Dream to be revealed and subsequently realized. As a result, instead of pursuing a Kingdom Dream, which was the plan, purpose and reason they were created, they pursue a carnal dream. In short, because they don't seek God, through seeking His way and His will, they miss fulfilling their God-given destiny.

It's important, therefore, to be able to distinguish between true Kingdom Dreams and carnal dreams. Later, I will spend considerable time doing just that. For now, let me emphasize that unlike Kingdom Dreams—which find their origins in God's will—carnal dreams are an outflow of people's wills and the worldly desires in their hearts. Unfortunately, most of what we hear preached from contemporary pulpits, and consequently most of what we see role-modeled by 21st Century Christians, are people living out their carnal dreams instead of embracing their Kingdom Dreams.

You see, what most of us have never been taught is that Satan is on our side.

Now I know you may be rubbing your eyes and wondering if you just read what you thought you read.

Yes, you did.

You need to know that the primary way Satan keeps many of us from fulfilling God's powerful purpose for our lives is by encouraging us to pursue our own pleasures and desires. Remember when Jesus told Peter He had to die on the cross? Peter rebuked Jesus and told Him that he would never let Him be crucified. The reason Peter was so angry with Jesus was that, in that moment, God's will conflicted with Peter's desires. But notice whose side Satan was on:

Jesus turned and said to Peter, "Get behind me, Satan! You are a stumbling block to me; you do not have in mind the things of God, but the things of men" (Matthew 16:23).

Jesus recognized how Satan was tempting Peter in that moment by simply agreeing with and encouraging him. This is the same way he tricked Eve in the garden; he encouraged her desire to indulge in her own pleasures. This is how he is going to try to trip you up, too; he is going to attempt to convince you that you can have God's will and your will at the same time. The Bible, however, never teaches us that we can do our God-given assignment and pursue our own pleasures simultaneously. It is a man-made philosophy to think that you can have it all. Jesus declared in the garden of Gethsemane, "... *Nevertheless, not my will, but yours, be done*" (Luke 22:42 ESV).

The fact is that many Christians have never stopped to consider what the Scripture has to say concerning their purpose and destiny. This, unfortunately, has resulted in many individuals pursuing goals and aspirations that neither reflect the plan of God nor bring glory to His name. You must look to the teachings of the Bible as the primary source for discovering your Kingdom Dream.

When you and I discard good, sound Biblical teaching, we give way to secularism, which is the act of thinking and living in a godless and worldly manner. Sadly, secularism has become extremely pervasive in the church. Most of the philosophies that today's Christians allow to shape their lives run counter to the teachings of Christ. For example, many are taught that happiness is more important than holiness, but Jesus clearly taught:

What good will it be for a man if he gains the whole world, yet forfeits his soul? Or what can a man give in exchange for his soul? (Matthew 16:26)

How can this erroneous secular philosophy prevent a Christian from accomplishing God's will? Say you have been dating someone for close to two years, and after a time of prayer you discover it is God's will for the two of you to get married. In obedience to God, you get married, but six months later you begin to have challenges and disagreements. Your spouse complains about how you spend money, and you aren't happy with the lack of attention and time given to you. You both have habits that deeply irritate the other, which leads to frequent arguments and a deep-rooted disappointment.

Discontentment begins to grow in your heart, and some of your secular-minded Christian friends advise you to leave the marriage because you seem so dissatisfied, and after all, God wants you to be happy. So convinced are you that your friends are right, you file for a divorce and leave the person God had called you to marry.

What you didn't know is that long before you were ever born, God shaped His plan for your life, and that plan included this person you were to marry. Although this person wasn't perfect, God knew that if you trusted Him and worked hard at honoring Him by staying committed to your marriage, one day you would discover your spouse was the perfect fit for you. In His plan for your life, you and your spouse were ordained to start a ministry together that would spread the Gospel to people all over the world and lead thousands to Jesus Christ. But because you wanted happiness over holiness, you forfeited God's Kingdom Dream for your life.

There are, without question, two legitimate, Biblically justifiable reasons permitted in Scripture for a divorce: marital unfaithfulness (Matthew 19:9) and the scenario the Apostle Paul addresses in 1 Corinthians 7:15, in which an unbelieving spouse desires to depart from a marriage to a Christian. There are also certain situations that are not directly addressed in Scripture that are more complicated and deserve serious consideration, such as the case of a marriage scarred by domestic abuse in the form of physical violence. However, there is absolutely no Biblical or theological support found in the teachings of Jesus or His Apostles for leaving a marriage simply because one is unhappy.

This is why we have to devote ourselves to the study and application of God's Word. The Bible acts as the road map for your Kingdom Dream, and without doctrinal correctness, you most likely will never arrive at His intended destination for your life. I urge you to become a diligent student of Scripture and theology. I also strongly recommend you seek out a church that provides excellent Biblical training. Don't settle for a ministry that simply inspires you; look for one that informs you as well. Your Kingdom Dream will only be as strong as the theology it is established upon.

As a pastor, I am committed to ensuring that the members of the church whom God has entrusted to my care are taught the truths of Scripture in a clear and uncompromised way. This isn't always easy, but I have chosen to honor God and resist the temptation to preach popular man-made philosophies. I do this because I have a passion to see every member of my congregation walking in their true Kingdom Dream and not wasting their lives pursuing meaningless carnal dreams. I am driven by the passage found in 2 Timothy 4:2-5:

Preach the Word; be prepared in season and out of season; correct, rebuke and encourage—with great patience and careful instruction. For the time will come when men will not put up with sound doctrine. Instead, to suit their own desires, they will gather around them a great number of teachers to say what their itching ears want to hear. They will turn their ears away from the truth and turn aside to myths. But you, keep your head in all situations, endure hardship, do the work of an evangelist, discharge all the duties of your ministry.

I want to drive home the thought that God decided to select you to fulfill a special purpose before the world began. The Bible and its writers develop this truth progressively as Scripture unfolds. This clearly is part of the mystery the Apostle Paul states was entrusted to him in Ephesians 1. The fact is that you were chosen by God!

I urge you not to move too quickly past that thought but to meditate on its profoundness: you were chosen by God! Maybe you were like me growing up and were never chosen for much. Maybe, like me, you experienced the scene at the baseball diamond when two captains formed their teams by choosing players. How embarrassing it was to be the smallest guy there and watch as one player after another was picked, but not you. Your heart began to race as you silently prayed not to be the last one chosen, because the last one chosen was not really chosen but simply placed on a team by default.

Never doubt that when it comes to your salvation, you don't have to feel any embarrassment. God proudly chose you.

Jesus is the captain of our salvation. When He was forming the team that would assist Him in His plan to redeem humanity, He looked over the billions of human souls that would populate the earth and, with love in His heart, saw you and said, "I want this one to be on my team." This one fact alone is enough to cause Satan to hate you eternally; God chose you but rejected him.

Jesus declared in the Gospel of John 15:16:

"You did not choose me, but I chose you..."

This statement, among many others, establishes firmly that God specially selected you as part of His awesome plan. Most Christians were never taught this; therefore, they don't understand the deep ramifications of this truth. The Apostle Paul went on to declare in Ephesians 1:4:

For he chose us in him before the creation of the world...

This means that before you did anything at all—right or wrong, good or bad—God, in His grace, decided He was going to love you and choose you to fulfill a special purpose on His behalf.

He clearly communicates this wonderful truth in Ephesians 2:10:

For we are God's workmanship, created in Christ Jesus to do good works, which God prepared in advance for us to do.

What all these Scriptures are teaching is that before time began, God decreed that He was going to save you and use you in a special way to accomplish certain good works on His behalf. I will soon dissect this thought further, but for now, consider this one fact: God did not choose everyone. There are some that God, because of reasons known only to Him, chooses not to redeem. Scripture bears this truth out in passages like Romans 9:15-18:

For he says to Moses, "I will have mercy on whom I have mercy, and I will have compassion on whom I have compassion." It does not, therefore, depend on man's desire or effort, but on God's mercy. For the Scripture says to Pharaoh: "I raised you up for this very purpose, that I might display my power in you and that my name might be proclaimed in all the earth." Therefore God has mercy on whom he wants to have mercy, and he hardens whom he wants to harden.

God wants you to understand and embrace that part of what makes you so blessed is that God's hand is upon you. And it is His selection of you that testifies of His love and purpose for your life.

Let me illustrate it this way. Say I was playing a game of pool, and on the pool table was the cue ball and a regulation set of pool balls, half solid and half striped. Now let's say I determined that my objective was to knock all of one set of balls into the pockets on the table. In order to maintain my integrity, I should declare before the game which set of balls I was shooting for, right? I pronounced my choice: the solids.

In God's plan, these solid balls act as the group of sinners whom God specifically chooses to save through His son Jesus Christ. The striped balls, therefore, act as the group of sinners whom He decides not to save. Although I'm not aiming for the striped balls, they still play an important role in assisting me in getting the solids in the pockets and winning the game. Likewise, in God's plan, even the unsaved play a role in assisting the salvation of those selected beforehand.

For example, many times God will use an unsaved boss on your job or an unsaved family member to challenge you in order to develop within you qualities such as mercy, forgiveness, and resilience. So you see, both the unchosen striped balls and the chosen solid balls are important to God's plan.

It's important to note that neither set of balls had any choice in how it would be used. The solid balls couldn't brag that their personal attractiveness led me to choose them, nor could the striped balls say it was unfair that I didn't choose them because they were just as attractive as the solid balls. No, through my own wisdom and for reasons known only to me, I made my own selection, and once it was made, my choice automatically became unchangeable.

Therefore, all the solid balls could do was rejoice in being selected, do all they could to fulfill my purpose for choosing them, and do all they could to express their appreciation for being selected. This is the reality that Scripture bears out, and this is the reality we must all embrace.

Like those pool balls you, too, were selected—not to roll into pool pockets, but as God's chosen people picked to play a critical role in His divine plan to bring glory to Himself. In my pool analogy, the only way I can get glory is by knocking all the solid balls into the pockets. As long as there is at least one solid remaining on the table, I can receive no glory. Likewise, the only way God receives glory is when all the sinners whom He predestined to be saved have heard and accepted the message of the redemption that Jesus Christ alone provides. It is to this end that you have been saved.

When you properly understand this teaching, it should provoke you to ask two very important questions: First, "what is my unique purpose within God's plan to redeem lost humanity?" and second, "what can I do to express my deep appreciation and gratitude for being chosen?" These are the two key questions that drive us to discover our Kingdom Dream. Not until we ask ourselves these two basic questions can we truly begin the journey to unveiling God's Kingdom Dream for our lives.

The Two BIG Questions

Theological doctrine can seem difficult to understand at best, but at the foundational level, it's quite simple: God's sovereign selection of you should drive you toward answering these two BIG questions of life.

Let's deal with the first question: "what is my unique purpose within God's plan to redeem lost humanity?" Whether we readily accept this or not, ultimately all of us, no matter how small or great, play some role in the redeeming of humanity. This is not a job that is just left up to the pastor or evangelist, as one who has been chosen this is part of the purpose for which we are born again. As instructed in 2 Timothy 4:5:

But watch thou in all things, endure afflictions, do the work of an evangelist, make full proof of thy ministry.

31

It's just part of the package. As Christians we are also commanded to pray, worship, and share our faith. But in addition to those very important things, there are also some unique good works that YOU specifically were created to accomplish. Jesus declares in John 17:4 (NIV):

I have brought you glory on earth by completing the work you gave me to do.

Notice that Jesus brought the Father glory by completing the unique assignment He had been given. Jesus didn't waste time trying to accomplish anyone else's assignment; he concentrated on his own. Likewise, you must not waste your life trying to be and do what God has assigned someone else to be or do. Whatever that special thing is, whether it is a Pastor, Fire Chief, Entrepreneur, Sunday School Teacher or President of the United States, you can only glorify God and be totally fulfilled in life when you seek with all your heart to discover your unique assignment within His Kingdom.

That unique good work that God selected and created you to accomplish on His behalf, is what I call your Kingdom Dream. What makes it so awesome is that, in His foreknowledge, God has already placed within you a desire to fulfill this unique assignment. When you discover what it is, you will know it, because your spirit will bear witness. You must start, though, by asking yourself that first big question.

Answering the first BIG Question, should lead you to the second BIG question: "What can I do to express my deep appreciation and gratitude for being chosen?" Now that you know that He has chosen you, you should use all your creativity, imagination, and gifts to express to Him how deeply you appreciate the fact that He chose you. It will take you an entire lifetime, but you should use all of your resources to show God how much you love Him. The greatest blessing in all of life is knowing Him, and knowing that you have been chosen by God to serve Him in this lifetime and to fellowship with Him for eternity. This is your dual quest: to discover His unique assignment for your life, and to express your gratitude for being chosen. Doing this will unlock God's Kingdom Dream for your life.

And that is exactly why you were chosen by God.

Kingdom Dream Devotional

Devotional Passage

...then the Lord knows how to deliver the godly out of temptations and to reserve the unjust under punishment for the day of judgment, and especially those who walk according to the flesh in the lust of uncleanness and despise authority. They are presumptuous, self-willed. They are not afraid to speak evil of dignitaries (2 Peter 2: 9, 10).

Kingdom Question

How well do you do at expressing your appreciation to God for all that He has done in your life?

Dream Development Exercise

Share with someone each day for the next week some of the wonderful things God has done in your life. Your testimony should include three parts:
- Who you were before you came to Christ
- How you met Christ
- Who you are now that you know Christ

3

It's Time to Dream Again!

*"When the Lord brought back the captives to Zion,
we were like men who dreamed."* (Psalms 126:1)

Ask most people what, as children, they wanted to be when they grew up, and you will see something strange begin to happen. A smile will form on their faces, and their eyes will begin to gaze joyfully off into the distance. They may even chuckle as they reminisce about the youthful optimism they once called their childhood dream. After thinking for a moment, their responses will often surprise you; some will downright astonish you. You will hear answers like "I wanted to be a singer," or, "I wanted to be an inventor." Some will say they wanted to be a doctor or the President of the United States.

Sadly, if you go on to ask those same people what their dreams are now that they're adults, you will see something strange begin to happen again. The smile that had earlier appeared on their faces will slowly fade, and their eyes will shift from a joyful gaze to a somber fixation as they, in slight frustration, respond with an ambiguous, "I'm not sure!" If you were to probe a little deeper and ask them what happened to their childhood dreams, the responses would most likely be something like: "I gave up on those a long time ago."

This is one of the most alarming realities of life: somewhere along the line, most people stop dreaming. There are normally three moments in life that, if we're not careful, will spell death to our dreams.

The first moment most of us stop dreaming is when we receive our first report card. You remember your first report card, don't you? The fact is that if you are like the average person, you probably omitted this day from your memories. But this is a day that should be considered again because of the major impact it had on our lives. You see, for most of us, the day of our first report card was the day our dreams began to die. This was the day we realized we weren't perfect. This was the day we realized that not everyone thought of us like Mom did. This was the sad day we realized that life was hard, and that dreams take a lot more than hope and fantasy. They require hard work and diligence.

The second moment we stopped dreaming is when we experienced our first major public embarrassment. How humiliating it was to stumble and fall in front of all of those other children on the playground, or to be caught daydreaming when the teacher called your name for the answer to the question on the board. Kids can be cruel; their laughter in situations like these can seem loud enough to wake a city and strong enough to break your little heart. Their mean-spirited eyes were all directed toward you as they peppered you with hurtful jokes and insults. All your mind could think was, "I wish I could disappear and never come back again." You see, this was the day you realized how painful failure could feel. This was the moment you were awakened to the fact that one missed step could cause a lifetime of scarred emotions. This was the day that many of us decided it was best to play it safe and not take too many risks, because risks could cause you to fall, and failure brings harsh consequences.

The final moment in which many of us allowed our dreams to die was the first time we liked someone and they didn't like us back. Many of us remember being in class and passing the note that read, "I like you, do you like me? Check yes or no!" We put our emotions on the line, and our heart was hanging in the balance. What a crushing blow to receive the response we weren't prepared to handle. This was the moment we realized rejection is bitter and cold. This was the day we decided it was better not to love than to risk loving and experience rejection. This was a day a small part of our dream began to die.

You see, for most of us, it is our inadequacies and fear of embarrassment and rejection that cause us to stop dreaming. As a result, we conform to the rest of the world around us. We settle for what report cards and guidance counselors tell us. We allow our fears of being mocked and ridiculed to talk us out of our dreams, and we become content with being average. We strive to not make waves. Our goal is to survive day by day and stay out of trouble. This persistence on being average and living a mediocre lifestyle kills our imagination and causes our dreams to die.

If you combine all this with the fact that our sinful nature leads us down pathways far from God, you have a recipe for death. Sin absolutely kills our ability to dream Godly dreams, and that is exactly what happens to the best of us. Our fears and sins combine to produce the death of our hopes, the death of our creativity, and the death of our dreams. Instead of being an awesome original, we exchange our uniqueness for being a carbon copy of someone else whom the masses have accepted, or we become a shadow of who we could have been if we simply trusted God.

What you have to realize is that this was Satan's plan from the beginning. His hope was to drive all of the imaginative power that God placed in you, out of you. His plan is that you would

become a prisoner to your fears, inadequacies, and sinfulness. This is why Satan's desire for you is that you would get yourself so entangled with adultery, addictions, and lies that your dreams would become a slave to these deadly behaviors and philosophies. Satan knows slaves don't dream.

If Satan can't get you to become a slave to your fears, he'll do his best to have you become a slave to the opinion of others. Starting in your youth, Satan's desire is to convince you that what is most important is what others think about you. Once many of us reach our adolescent years, we are so desperate for acceptance that we are willing to compromise our self-image and self-worth. For far too many, this approval addiction extends into adulthood. We spend tons of money on makeup, designer clothes, and external accessories, all in hopes of winning the approval of the masses. Without even knowing it, we become slaves to the opinions and images of the world around us. Once you become imprisoned by the fickle judgments of the shallow people you have allowed to critique you, your dreams will begin to die. Remember: slaves don't dream!

Slaves don't believe they can become President. Slaves don't believe they can become great scholars, and slaves have no idea that one day God could use them so mightily that a whole generation would be changed through their influence and wisdom. No, the fact is,

slaves don't dream. The Bible declares in John 8:34:

Jesus replied, "I tell you the truth, everyone who sins is a slave to sin."

Scripture goes on in 2 Peter 2:19 to declare that:

...a man is a slave to whatever has mastered him.

What have you allowed to master you? What have you allowed to dominate or control your thinking, actions, and beliefs? This is the very thing that has taken you captive and stolen you away from God and His loving plan for your life. It's time for you to be delivered. Jesus Christ has come to set you free. He doesn't want you to be a slave anymore to the opinions of others or to the bondage of sin, or even to your own fears. Jesus knows that slaves don't dream.

This is why the Psalmist was so right when he wrote in Psalm 126, *"When the Lord brought back the captives from Zion, we were like men who dreamed."* Here God reminds us that dreams don't begin until freedom is realized. His desire is to bring you freedom and salvation from the fears and sin in your life.

So if the Son sets you free, you will be free indeed (John 8:36).

Jesus Christ died so that He might liberate your spirit and return to you the ability to dream. His presence in your life literally unleashes your capacity to dream Godly dreams. You must remember that, as a child of God, you were created in His image. God wanted you to be like Him. One of the greatest attributes of God is His ability to see what has not yet appeared. Likewise, God wants you to be able to see beyond your current limitations, circumstances, and challenges. He wants you to be able to dream of the possibilities that could happen if you allowed His power to work in and through you to change the world.

Our ability to see with our imaginations does not awaken until we are freed from the bondage of our fears and sinfulness. The truth is that when sin entered the picture, we regressed and gave up some of our Godliness. Theologians refer to this as the fall of man. We fell from the status and position God had reserved for us. In many ways, we forfeited the image of God in our lives. Sin causes us to no longer be like Him. Sin strips us of our ability to imagine possibilities beyond our current circumstances. Thanks be unto God because through Jesus Christ, we now have redemption and the restoration of our "godlikeness." We now can dream again.

One of the results of having the Holy Spirit poured out upon you is that you are going to begin to dream. The presence of the Holy Spirit in your life awakens your God-given ability to dream. Peter, when speaking on the day of Pentecost, put it this way:

In the last days, God says, I will pour out my Spirit on all people. Your sons and daughters will prophesy, your young men will see visions, your old men will dream dreams (Acts 2:17).

The Power of a Dream!

"If you can?" said Jesus. "Everything is possible for him who believes" (Mark 9:23).

Nothing empowers an individual more than believing. It is our faith in a person, objective, or aspiration that brings energy and focus to our lives. I want you to be clear and careful about what I am saying. Although I have deep convictions as a Christian about what is the right object of our faith, namely Jesus Christ, I am also very honest about the fact that belief in itself is powerful. Belief in a dream has the ability to transform us from directionless wanderers to concentrated, single-minded conquerors able to prevail over the greatest challenges life throws our way.

A study of human history will reveal that when a person or group determines to proactively place their faith in a goal, they become empowered in unimaginable ways, enabling them to accomplish great feats. One great example of this is the 1980 United States Olympic hockey team. This collection of amateur young men, ranging

42

from ages 18 to 22, defied all odds by defeating what was then labeled the most dominating hockey team of all time, the Russian Olympic team. These Russians were professional players who were so physically overpowering they were like gladiators on ice. Their towering success was a product of both their physical strength and sheer skill. For several decades, they manhandled and dominated the rest of the world in hockey. No one on earth ever imagined that they would be defeated on the world's biggest stage by a group of kids.

The movie *Miracle* recounts this tale of triumph and details the one factor that allowed the U.S. hockey team to be victorious against all odds. The fact is this group of nobodies, who seemed destined to be crushed by the far superior Russians, overcame because of their united belief. In what has to be one of the most amazing accounts of managerial motivation, their coach was successful in convincing this group of impressionable young men that if they worked together as a team, instead of a collection of talented individuals like the Russians, they would win. In other words, he empowered them by persuading them to put their faith in the fact that a highly disciplined team will always prevail over a group of talented individuals. And it worked! The U.S. team shocked the world and took home the gold.

Faith in a dream has a profoundly empowering effect on our lives. Our dreams enable us to accomplish otherwise impossible feats. A person who is driven by a dream is freed from the realm of limitations—which restrict so many of us—and becomes capable of achieving what was previously viewed as unattainable. A dream is so powerful because it literally strips us of our weaknesses and redefines what was once ridiculous as being reasonable and possible. Dreams transform us because they empower us in three key ways.

The first way in which our dreams empower us is by enabling us to live with passion. By definition, any goal provides you with direction. A person without a goal is simply wandering through life. Once we have a definite aspiration, we have something we can passionately pursue. No longer is life a repeat of the mundane; rather, it becomes an adventure. Waking up in the morning becomes a joy for the person who has discovered his or her dream. Sleeping becomes an inconvenient interruption, and laziness is replaced with unbridled motivation, when we are awakened to our Kingdom Dream.

The second way our dreams empower us is by providing us with the strength needed to overcome the obstacles of life. Take Pam, for instance. Pam was a young mother who had been feeling extremely fatigued for several weeks. Concerned about her health, she scheduled an appointment with her physician. What resulted was totally unexpected. She was sent through a battery of medical examinations, which ultimately revealed a rare and incurable blood disease. After exhausting all possible alternatives, the conclusions were undeniable. All that was left was the devastating pronouncement by the rather tactless specialist who bluntly told her she probably wouldn't live to see her sons' next birthdays. To this she responded, "I will live and not die." With resolve in her heart, she knew that the power of her dream to raise her two boys gave her more credentials in this matter than all the degrees and accreditations of the specialists standing before her prophesying doom. Pam went on to celebrate several of her sons' birthdays with vigor and vitality, and it was her dream that allowed her to look overwhelming challenges in the face and declare, "I will not be defeated."

Similarly, any time an individual or group fully embraces and internalizes a dream; it will provide them with the strength needed to defeat their challenges and their challengers. The nation of Israel has always been one of the smallest in the world. Jews make up less that 2% of the global population, and in Israel, they are surrounded by Arab nations who, for the most part, despise their existence and hope for their destruction. But from the time of Abraham and the patriarchs until today, Israel has been a story of triumph, because the Israelites are convinced that God has destined them to occupy their land. To them, it is the land of promise. To them, it is their dream. This is why this tiny nation has defied their enemies so many times.

The third way our dreams empower us is by providing us with the motivation to maximize our potential. One of the greatest thinkers, theologians and scholars that America has ever produced was Jonathan Edwards. A former president of Princeton University, Edwards mastered several languages before he died, authored numerous books, and was the catalyst for many organizations that have gone on to change our country. This is just a short list of his immeasurable accomplishments and impact on the world. Edwards was motivated by his dream to change the world for the cause of Christ. His passion for Christ was most clearly evident in a document he wrote called "The Resolutions of Jonathan Edwards."[1] This pledge of 70 commitments, written over the course of two years, contains vows Edwards made to advance the cause of Christ. These pledges still rank among the greatest declarations any individual has ever made to maximize and exhaust their potential.

The following records just a few of the decrees he promised to fulfill before he died:

Resolution #1 – Resolved, that I will do whatsoever I think to be most to God's glory, and my own good, profit and pleasure, in the whole and duration, without any consideration of the time, whether now, or never so many myriads of ages hence. Resolve to do whatever I think to be my duty and most for the good and advantage of mankind in general. Resolve to do this, whatever difficulties I meet with, how many and how great soever.

Resolution #5 – Resolved, never to lose one moment of time; but improve it the most profitable way I possibly can.

Resolution #6 – Resolved, to live with all my might, while I do live.

Resolution #11 – Resolved, when I think of any theorem in divinity to be solved, immediately to do what I can towards solving it, if circumstances don't hinder.

Resolution #17 – Resolved, that I will live so as I shall wish I had done when I come to die.

Resolution #20 – Resolved, to maintain the strictest temperance in eating and drinking.

Resolution #22 – Resolved, to endeavor to obtain for myself as much happiness, in the other world, as I possibly can, with all the power, might, vigor, and vehemence, yea violence, I am capable of, or can bring myself to exert, in any way that can be thought of.

Resolution #30 – Resolved, to strive to my

utmost every week to be brought higher in religion, and to a higher exercise of grace, than I was the week before.

Resolution #41 – Resolved, to ask myself, at the end of every day, week, month and year, wherein I could possibly in any respect have done better. [1]

Wow what passion! This humble and Godly man did everything within his power to maximize every ounce of his potential because of his dream to glorify God. Can you see how our dream can provide us the determination and willpower needed to make the most of our lives?

God wants you to dream because He knows there are certain things that only a dream can empower you to do. This is why, when God was calling Abraham, He took him out by night and gave him a mental image of all the stars in the sky as his future descendants:

The angel of the Lord called to Abraham from heaven a second time and said, "I swear by myself, declares the Lord, that because you have done this and have not withheld your son, your only son, I will surely bless you and make your descendants as numerous as the stars in the sky and as the

[1] Edwards, J. (1722). Jonathan Edwards' Resolutions. Retrieved September 28, 2007 from A Puritan's Mind: Christian Walk. http://www.apuritansmind.com/ChristianWalk/ ResolutionsOfJonathanEdwards.htm.

sand on the seashore. Your descendants will take possession of the cities of their enemies, and through your offspring all nations on earth will be blessed, because you have obeyed me (Genesis 22:15-18).

God used visual object lessons to awaken Abraham's imagination so that he might dream, knowing that his dreams would empower him to accomplish the great purpose for which God had called him. I could chronicle the lives of many of the great men and women we celebrate throughout human history, and at the foundation of their success we would find that it was their dreams that gave them the ability to live with passion, overcome seemingly overwhelming obstacles, and realize their full potential.

Kingdom Dream Devotional

Devotional Passage

Read the entire book of Romans.

Desiring to be teachers of the law; understanding neither what they say, nor whereof they affirm (1 Timothy 1:7).

Kingdom Question

What are some fears that have kept you from pursuing your Dream?

Dream Development Exercise

Make a list of at least 10 life resolutions you vow to keep in order to glorify God.

4

Carnal Dreams vs. Kingdom Dreams

Many are the plans in a man's heart, but it is the Lord's purpose that prevails (Proverbs 19:21).

It's important to remember that not all dreams are the same. As I alluded to earlier, there are two types of dreams a person can embrace. First, there are what I call carnal dreams, which are desires, goals, or aspirations that are selfish and worldly in nature. These plans are centered on self-promotion, prosperity, and happiness. These dreams rarely consider the glory of God or the needs of those around us. If God or others are considered, they are usually an afterthought, so marginalized that they have no tangible impact on how we live our lives.

Unfortunately, these are the only dreams many of us have ever imagined. Most of us have never dreamed outside of the realm of career goals, personal financial success, or expanding our own popularity. From the time we were young, we were taught that individual success is richly rewarded and self-sacrifice is often ignored. After all, there are very few banquets given to recognize the most humble servant, and very few trophies given to the meek or the mild. Everywhere we look, we are bombarded with images of self-promotion and egotism. These images are so popularized and branded into our consciousness, they can influence everything we do.

This is unfortunately true, even within Christian circles. The church seems to have forgotten what Paul taught:

> *In everything I did, I showed you that by this kind of hard work we must help the weak, remembering the words the Lord Jesus himself said: "It is more blessed to give than to receive."* (Acts 20:35)

It is almost as if the church by and large has exchanged her "giving" spirit for a "getting" spirit. Far too many Christians have allowed our society to impact them in negative ways that promote greed and selfishness. Ask yourself, "How many people do you know who are passionately driven by the selfless desire to help those who are helpless, poor, and needy?" If you are anything like me, the sad fact is that you don't know many believers who live this way. True, there are a lot of Christians who will claim that their motive is to help others. When you dig deeper, you often find that, underneath it all, their commitment will only remain as long as there is a positive effect for them financially, or as long as they can get public acknowledgement of their good deeds. Very few people suffer personally in order to see another person blessed. Even fewer forgo personal pleasures for the benefit of someone else's advancement if there is no guarantee they will get any public credit for it.

We have become so twisted in our theology of giving that many pastors teach their flocks that the motive behind giving is to get more. This has resulted in such spiritual carnality and impurity that we have a generation of carnal dreamers throughout the Body of Christ. But let me tell you this: there is a whole world of awesomely wonderful dreams that you have yet to tap into, dreams that are based totally on the promotion of God's glory throughout the earth.

These types of aims fall into the second category of dreams: the Kingdom Dreams, which share these three characteristics:

1. **God-centered:** the focus of Kingdom Dreams is to fulfill the individual God-given assignment for your life. Individuals who are Kingdom Dreamers are propelled by their goal to provoke

praise to the name of God in others. Everything about a Kingdom Dream is designed to please God and to bring Him greater glory.

2. **Evangelistic:** the nature of Kingdom Dreams is that they are deeply rooted in the kind of great compassion found in Matthew 28:19-20:

Therefore go and make disciples of all nations, baptizing them in the name of the Father and of the Son and of the Holy Spirit, and teaching them to obey everything I have commanded you. And surely I am with you always, to the very end of the age.

The passion of a Kingdom Dream is to see as many people as possible come to a saving knowledge of Jesus Christ. Kingdom Dreamers are convinced that the primary calling of God on their lives is to be a blessing to others who are hurting, broken, and in need of God's love. Kingdom Dreamers are persuaded that the greatest of all benefits one can render to others is the offer to make Jesus Christ the Lord of their life. Because of this, Kingdom Dreamers are extremely zealous about seeing others saved.

3. **Faith-sized:** Because Kingdom Dreams have their origin in God; we cannot accomplish them without His help and the help of other members of His body. True Kingdom Dreams demand

that we cooperate and unify with other Christians to achieve God's will for our lives. The fact is that the God we serve has a big vision for the world and for your life; therefore, your Kingdom Dream will most likely be large. Our dreams should force us to reach out to God and others.

Unlike carnal dreamers, Kingdom Dreamers possess the "giving" spirit of Jesus and not the "getting" spirit of the world. Kingdom Dreams cause us to die to ourselves and be reborn to God. Make no mistake about it, a Kingdom Dream will, in many ways, cause you to lose sight of yourself. But this is good—it ensures you will no longer be hindered by the impediments of self-promotion or ego, two of the greatest barriers to our being able to accomplish truly extraordinary feats on God's behalf. It's like one blind Christian once said:

The day that I lost my sight was the moment I gained my vision!

Jesus put it this way in Matthew 16:25:

For whoever wants to save his life will lose it, but whoever loses his life for me will find it.

It is not until we are willing to lose our lives in Jesus that we become Kingdom Dreamers. I know this may sound difficult, even impossible, but it is the only path to unveiling God's true desire for your life. Other paths are only attempts to somehow combine our will with His. This mixture of our selfish and sinful will with His divine and holy will only produces a muddled, convoluted, and watered-down purpose that acts as a dim shadow of the glorious plan God created us to accomplish. Remember that Jesus acts as our human example, and it was He who acknowledged the inadequacy of human attempts to combine our wills with God's when he cried out in his moment of testing:

> ...*O my Father, if it be possible, let this cup pass from me: nevertheless not as I will, but as thou wilt* (Matthew 26:39 KJV).

Jesus recognized the pointlessness in trying to combine human will with divine will. One must succumb to the other. If you desire to become a Kingdom Dreamer, your human will and desires must succumb to His divine will and plan.

Now take a moment to consider your present plan, the path you are currently on, and the goals that are driving you. Which category do your dreams fall under? Are your dreams deeply rooted and passionately driven by your desire to bring God glory, or are they simply focused on your personal happiness and worldly fulfillment? The answer to this question will reveal whether you are dreaming a carnal dream or a Kingdom Dream.

Why Kingdom Dreams are Superior to Carnal Dreams

Thus far in this chapter, I have explained the power that all dreams possess. Good or bad, right or wrong, all dreams empower us with the ability to live beyond our current circumstances and limitations. This is why Hitler could perform such detestably devastating acts of destruction that destroyed millions of lives on the one hand, and Mother Theresa could change the world through powerful acts of human kindness and compassion on the other.

All dreams are not equal in power. As a matter of fact, Scripture makes a strong argument for the superiority of Kingdom Dreams over carnal dreams. The Bible teaches us that God opposes the wicked and is on the side of the righteous. Because, by definition, Kingdom Dreams are focused on pleasing God, He richly pours out His grace and favor upon the Kingdom Dreamer. In other words, Kingdom Dreams are superior to carnal dreams for one great reason: they alone carry the full endorsement of God.

Scripture makes clear that God's hand is against the wicked and the proud, while He exalts the righteous and the humble. Because carnal dreamers refuse to give God glory, they evoke the wrath of God. Be clear that God is against our carnal dreams, just as he stood against those in Genesis 11 who desired to build a tower to reach the heavens. Their only desire was to exalt themselves to the highest levels and to compete with God for His majesty. As a result, God opposed them, confused their language, and scattered them across the face of the earth. This is the fate of carnal dreamers.

There are two reasons why God so richly blesses Kingdom Dreams. The first, which I have attempted to drive home throughout this chapter, is that they bring God the most glory. Kingdom Dreams expand God's name and fame throughout the earth. They promote the worship of Jesus Christ. They take the message of the Gospel to those who have not heard of the love of the Master. With this, God is well pleased.

Secondly, Kingdom Dreams receive God's endorsement because they do the most good for mankind. God loves His creation and all mankind. Even those who are in rebellion against or reject God still receive some outpouring of His mercy and grace every day. The Bible declares in Matthew 5:45:

He causes his sun to rise on the evil and the good, and sends rain on the righteous and the unrighteous.

Kingdom Dreamers are moved by the compassion and love of God to bless others. Kingdom Dreams not only benefit others spiritually, which again is the greatest of all ways we can benefit another person, but they also enrich a person's practical life. This is why some of the greatest doctors, inventors, and scientists have been Christians driven by their God-glorifying passion to bless others. God wants to see people saved and rescued from the pain inflicted upon them by Satan and the realities of living in a sinful world. He delivers those who are in bondage by blessing the Kingdom Dreams of His people.

I encourage you today to become a Kingdom Dreamer. Dare to dream something that is focused upon bringing the maximum glory to God and the greatest good to humanity. Don't be afraid to be boldly different than most others around you. It is this difference in thinking and desire that makes you unique. It is your desire to live totally for the Master that makes you free and allows you to dream Godly dreams. It is your willingness to express your gratitude to the Lord for choosing you to be His that secures God's full endorsement for your Kingdom Dream!

Kingdom Dream Devotional

Devotional Passage

...that I may know Him and the power of His resurrection, and the fellowship of His sufferings, being conformed to His death, if, by any means, I may attain to the resurrection from the dead.

Pressing Toward the Goal

Not that I have already attained, or am already perfected; but I press on, that I may lay hold of that for which Christ Jesus has also laid hold of me. Brethren, I do not count myself to have apprehended; but one thing I do, forgetting those things which are behind and reaching forward to those things which are ahead, I press toward the goal for the prize of the upward call of God in Christ Jesus (Philippians 3:10-14).

Kingdom Question

What dreams will you have to give up in order to accomplish your Kingdom Dream?

Dream Development Exercise

Pray and ask God what group of people he would have you to serve and reach on His behalf and make a list of three ways you can bless them.

5

The King's Dream!

And we know that in all things God works for the good of those who love him, who have been called according to his purpose (Romans 8:28).

One of the most annoying inventions ever created and forced upon humanity has to be the alarm clock. Think about it. How many times has a wonderful morning been rudely interrupted by the ringing of an unforgiving alarm clock on your night stand? How many sweet dreams have come to an abrupt end all because your clock decided you were clearly enjoying yourself far too much and resting far too well? As difficult as it may be to admit, however, the alarm clock's value far exceeds its drawbacks. I must humbly confess that there have been a lot of important meetings, beneficial relationships, and dynamic opportunities I would have missed if it were not for my alarm clock. If you think about it, we should thank God for alarm clocks, because they wake us up to blessings that we would have slept our way through had they not been so loud and upsetting.

In many ways, God places people in our lives to act as human alarm clocks. I hope I'm one of yours. I hope the message I've been sharing over the pages of the preceding chapters has come through loud and clear, shocking you into a new reality. I know that some of the concepts we have covered so far in this book can be challenging and difficult, maybe a bit inconvenient. After all, being told that you can no longer pursue self-centered goals, and that every aspiration of your life has to be totally focused upon bringing God glory may be an annoying truth to accept or feel like a goal too gigantic to even attempt. Truth, nonetheless, is exactly what it is, and truth is the only thing that can wake us up out of the spiritual sleep that we so often find ourselves in.

I hope that, so far, I have successfully used the truths of God's Word to awaken you to the fact that it is time for you to dream again! I pray that you have risen from the slumber of simply dreaming carnal dreams to the awesome life that comes when you allow your imagination to visualize the amazing life God has equipped you to lead in order to bring Him glory. It's time to wipe the sleep from your eyes and resist the intoxicating melodies of the world and our culture. Satan's greatest desire is to tempt you into becoming one of the sleeping masses, wasting life away, unaware that God created them to change the world on His behalf.

What I'm saying is: WAKE UP! It's time you wake up to the Kingdom Dream that God has placed in you and ordained, before the world began, that you would accomplish. Wake up to the passion of pursuing His glory with all of your being, and to proclaiming Him to all who will listen. Wake up to the life that God has always intended for you to live. Wake up to the empowering grace God has given you to change the world forever.

Stop hitting the snooze button! You can't afford to wait another year, another month, or another day—not even another minute! You have to begin to step out in faith and obedience and say "yes" to the call of God right now. Stop taking the sleeping medication of days gone by and embrace the urgency of right now. Choose to start living the life God has destined for you to live. Choose to awaken the Kingdom Dream that lies dormant within you.

Let the Holy Spirit Jump-Start Your Life!

Growing up in Michigan, I learned a lot about cold winters and freezing temperatures. Because of this, I also realize how important it is to make sure your car has a strong battery. One of the worst winter experiences a person can have is to walk through a windy parking lot in single-degree weather only to get to a car that refuses to turn over and start. Unfortunately, I have had the displeasure of this happening to me on several occasions.

Far worse than having a dead battery in your car, though, is having a dead battery in your life.

Have you ever told someone that you were burned out, had become emotionally numb, or had lost your passion for life? This is no different than saying your battery has died. Anytime you find it hard to turn over in the morning or accomplish the day's tasks, odds are you have a dead battery. What's the best option for recharging a dead battery? Get a boost, of course, from someone whose battery is fully charged and far more powerful than yours.

When it comes to your spiritual life, the Holy Spirit is that battery, and your faith in God acts as the jumper cables you need to tap into the fullness of His life. If you can believe that God has a tremendous plan for your life and that He wants to use you to leave an indelible impression upon the world, then you will begin to be recharged.

Kingdom Dreams recharge our life batteries after they have gone dead due to the stress, pain, and disappointments of the cold winters life sometimes brings our way. Our Kingdom Dreams recharge us because they connect us to the very heart of God, our power source. God's plan for your life is your Kingdom Dream. In fact, a proper understanding of Scripture reveals that at the center of God's heart is His dream to save the world through His Son Jesus Christ. The moment we tap into this dream (or what I call our King's Dream) by using the jumper cables of our faith, we are able to experience His life flowing through us.

I know this is contrary to what the world has taught us. It is hard to believe that our dreams will come alive as we get excited about someone else's dream. But this is exactly how it works in God's Kingdom. The reason your dreams will come alive when you get passionate about them is that you and God have an eternal connection. Just like fish are eternally connected to water and plants are eternally connected to soil, so you and I (human beings) are eternally connected to God. In other words, if you remove a fish from water, it will die. Likewise, if you remove a plant from soil, it, too, will surely die. In the same manner, when we become disconnected from God, we begin a process of slow death. This is what is happening to most of the people you see around you; they are slowly dying and gradually losing their enthusiasm for living, their vision for the future, and their dream for their lives. They are accepting the death of simply surviving.

Child of God, the way you bring life back to a dying fish is to reconnect it to water, and the way you bring life back to a dying plant is to reconnect it with soil. Therefore, it should be of no surprise that the way you bring life back to a person whose dreams have died is to reconnect them to the heart of God. This is what Peter was referring to in John 6:66-69 in his dialogue with Jesus. Scripture records the following conversation:

> *From this time many of his disciples turned back and no longer followed him. "You do not want to leave too, do you?" Jesus asked the Twelve. Simon Peter answered him, "Lord, to whom shall we go? You have the words of eternal life. We believe and know that you are the Holy One of God."*

Peter was convinced that his only hope for life was to stay connected to Jesus. He was persuaded that everything he had been searching for in life was wrapped up in knowing Christ. He believed that the more he surrendered his life to God's plan, the more he would come alive to his own purpose. From that day on, he set himself on a journey to become a Kingdom Dreamer. His goal was no longer to become the best fisherman in Galilee, but rather to become the greatest fisher of men in God's Kingdom. When he discovered his King's Dream, he found his own dream, and his life finally began to make sense to him and become worth living. The reason you need to seek your King's Dream is that once you discover it, your life will make sense, and the joy of living will fill every day.

Your God has a dream, and He wants to share it with you. Not only does He want to share His dream with you, He also wants to bless you by showing you what your role is within His dream. And He promises you that the very peace, joy, love, and fulfillment you have been searching for all of your life will be found inside of His dream. If you are willing to connect with God by faith, you will be infused with the power of God's purpose for your life.

The Lord is looking for individuals whose hearts are eager to do His will. He is seeking those who are willing to die to their own self-interest and live by His Spirit, yearning only to fulfill His desire. All those who possess an unselfish ear have the ability to hear the Lord as He pours out His heart for His plan to save that which is lost.

Have You Ever Listened to God?

I remember waking up one morning, not too long ago, to pray. It was so early that my wife and daughter were still sound asleep. In many ways, it was the perfect time to commune with the Lord. I found a quiet place in my house and began, as I normally do, to share with God all of my concerns, issues, and struggles. I earnestly requested His help in all the matters that were heaviest upon my heart. I felt it had been a wonderful time of fellowship with the Lord. But as I was ending my time of prayer, I felt the Holy Spirit ask me a question: "Do you want to know what is on my heart this morning?"

Though His voice was as loving and gentle as any I had ever heard, His words were piercing and painful, exposing the selfishness of my character. Here I had spent more than 30 minutes with my God and King, the lover of my soul, and the Savior of my life, and I had never stopped to ask Him what He wanted to talk about! With a heavy heart, I apologized and said, "Yes, Lord, I do want to know what's on your heart this morning!" For the next hour, He spoke to me about things that were not even on my radar; what He revealed to me, I hadn't even known I was searching for. And He blessed me in ways I hadn't expected and never imagined.

I wonder what would happen if you simply asked God what was on His heart, then sat and listened. This may seem awkward and uncomfortable at first, but be patient, because He will speak. Remember that the Scripture declares in John 10:27:

My sheep listen to my voice; I know them, and they follow me.

If you listen closely enough, you will hear God pour out His heart to you in the same way He spoke to me. He will tell you the answers to questions you didn't even know you had, as well as give you peace about the issues you have been wrestling with for so long. But do you know what else? If you listen to Him—and I mean truly, sincerely, and deeply listen to Him as He shares His deepest desires with you—you will discover that God has a dream He wants you to embrace. Your King has a dream in His heart for His creation, which He has been trying to reveal to man since the beginning of time. God has a dream, and He wants to tell you about it. Are you listening?

Too many of us are so wrapped up in talking to God about our issues that we are unable to hear Him when He wants to tell us what's important to Him. The fact of the matter is that the primary purpose of prayer is not for us to present all of our wants and requests to him, though He does permit us to do so. Instead, the primary purpose of prayer is for us to allow God to shape our hearts and wills to fit His. He shapes us by speaking to us about His plan for our lives. This is why I decided long ago to spend more time listening in my moments of prayer than I do talking. After all, He is the one with all the answers, so it is far more beneficial for me to simply listen to Him as He directs and guides my heart towards His.

God's Plan for the World

Therefore go and make disciples of all nations, baptizing them in the name of the Father and of the Son and of the Holy Spirit, and teaching them to obey everything I have commanded you. And surely I am with you always, to the very end of the age (Matthew 28: 19-23).

There is a big secret that Satan has been fighting hard for you not to discover. Satan's worst nightmare is the thought of you awakening and becoming excited about God's plan for the world. This is what he has been trying to distract you from with all the lust of the world and the pride of life. He has used every tactic he could to keep you from this moment. This is the day he has feared from the time of your birth. He knows that if you can embrace what I am about to share with you, there is no hope for him to have any more control over your life. His lies will be rendered ineffective, and his tricks will become powerless. He doesn't want you to know your King's Dream, but it's too late—God has been drawing your heart to His so strongly that nothing the enemy tried to do in your past was capable of keeping you from this moment. And here it is: Your King's Dream!

God's dream can be summarized in what is known as the Great Commission. Just prior to His departure,

Jesus left final instructions for His followers. These instructions act as the mission statement for all believers throughout all time. And they are quite clear. Simply put, God wants to expand His Kingdom. He wants as many carbon copies of Jesus as possible throughout the earth. God is looking for men and women who will be Christ-like in their attitudes, actions, and lifestyles. What is most exciting is that He want you and me to assist Him in getting His message out to the world. If we are willing to do this, He promises us that He will pour out His favor, grace, and blessings upon us.

Our involvement in the fulfilling of the Great Commission is clearly defined when Jesus gives the directive to "go and make disciples." As we will examine further, the making of disciples is the Great Commission. This is to say that the Great Commission is not compromised of several different commands, but one singular thrust, if you will, and that is to go and make disciples. Everything else that follows simply acts as supporting instructions for how we are to make disciples. The meaning of the term disciple is "a person who is striving to become Christ-like in every aspect of their life." What the Lord wants is for the world to be populated with men and women who are Christ-like and impacting their communities on behalf of the Kingdom of God. In light of this, let's reexamine Romans 8:29:

For those God foreknew he also predestined to be conformed to the likeness of his Son, that he might be the firstborn among many brothers.

Jesus was sent into the world both to redeem men unto God through His death and to be a role model, showing men how to truly be sons of God. He shows us how to love and obey the Father through the life that He lived. After He died and was resurrected, He commanded us to go and do as He had done and live for the Father. In addition, He charged us with the responsibility to think beyond ourselves and to do all that we can to encourage others to join us in our quest to become disciples of Christ.

God was so pleased with Christ, that He desires more men and women to live like He did. Jesus tells us repeatedly in the Gospels that He always pleases the Father. Scripture even declares in the Gospel of John 5:19 that Jesus only did what He saw the Father doing. This means that He was perfectly obedient in serving the Father and did all He could to glorify God, all His life. This is how God wants us to live and, more importantly, how He wants us to encourage others to live. He wants us to be disciple-makers.

How to Make a Disciple

As we unwrap the Father's desire for more Christ-like men and women (more disciples), we can clarify the King's Dream. Furthermore, the better we understand the King's Dream, the more precisely we will be able to see our unique role within His dream, which will bring us to a more prefect understanding of our own Kingdom Dream. Please don't miss this point because it is vital for your success. All too often we want to jump to the end game or final destination. After all, who wants to go through the process when we can have the finished product? But remember that in God's eyes the process is just as important as the finished product. This is why it is critical for you to know that the process for your discovering and fulfilling God's dream for your life is for you to deeply understand His plan for the world, or what I call your King's Dream.

Earlier I explained that the Great Commission can be summed up in one clear directive: "go and make disciples." But how do you and I make disciples? How can we change a man or woman who doesn't know Christ, and is not interested in living for Christ, into a person whose greatest pursuit is to become Christ-like in every aspect of their life? This task seems not only daunting, but flat-out overwhelming.

However, Jesus will never give you a commandment without providing you the tools and instructions needed to satisfy the requirements of that commandment. Christ provides us with two supportive instructions to the command to "go and make disciples," both found in Matthew 28:19. These two supportive instructions act as Jesus' recipe for disciple-making. The first comes when He says to His followers:

...baptizing them in the name of the Father and of the Son and of the Holy Spirit...

In other words, the first step to making disciples is to introduce them to Jesus. The instruction given here is for us to baptize people into the Body of Christ. In the early days of the Christian movement, baptism was another way of speaking of someone's conversion to Christ. When Jesus told His followers to go into the world and baptize men and women into the body, they would have clearly understood this to be an instruction to preach the Gospel and share their faith.

This is why all Kingdom Dreams must be evangelistic in nature. If we are going to fulfill the King's Dream, we must strive to do all we can to share our faith with as many people as we possibly can. The expectation of Jesus is that we would use all our creativity, imagination, and charisma to proclaim the message of Christ to our generation.

Jesus promised that anyone who followed after Him would play a key role in the fulfillment of the King's Dream. In many ways, He wanted every Christian to understand that we all have a unique place in God's plan to reach and redeem humanity. This is important for you to understand, because many believers feel that it's not their job to win the lost or share their faith with others. Some are convinced that all they are required to do is go to church and try to live a good and moral life. We have been taught that it is the pastor's job to win the lost, but this is simply not true. Every Christian has his or her own role within the King's Dream; this means we all must play our part in introducing men to the Savior of the world. Child of God, every one of us has a Kingdom Dream, and every one of us must assist the Father in His desire to redeem mankind. Look at what Jesus said in Matthew 4:19:

> *"Come, follow me," Jesus said, "and I will make you fishers of men."*

This is our job in life once we become Christians. We are to catch human fish for God. In other words, we are to share the message of the Gospel, teaching the world that:

> *God so loved the world that he gave his one and only son, that whoever believes in him shall not perish but have eternal life* (John 3:16).

We must announce God's love and grace to everyone who will listen, because this is our King's Dream. But we can't stop with just preaching.

The second ingredient Jesus gives us for making a disciple is seen again in the Great Commission of Matthew 28 when He says:

... and teaching them to obey everything I have commanded you.

Here Jesus' specific instruction to His followers is that we are called to proclaim to the world not only that Christ saves, but that He has taught us how the Father expects us to live our lives. Jesus knows that the two ingredients needed to make a disciple are first to get them saved by sharing the Gospel with them, and second to teach them how to live saved. There are two ways to teach others, informally and through formal instruction. Most teaching happens informally as we hold casual conversations with new converts to the faith about how the teachings of Christ apply to real-life situations. When we teach through formal times of classroom instruction, we expound upon what the Bible has to say about living for God. Both are very important and vital for producing a true disciple.

Jesus spent His entire earthly ministry explaining how God the Father has commanded us to carry ourselves in this world. What Jesus specifically taught was that we don't have the right to choose our own lifestyles, but rather we ought to seek out His teachings so that we can live in a manner which pleases the Father.

Again, as we seek to discover our own unique Kingdom Dream, we must keep the Father's "big picture" goal in mind. His dream is for us to reproduce Christ in ourselves and others. If we are going to make a disciple, we have to reeducate men and women concerning what they have been taught about how to live their lives. Equally important is being a role model to show them how to contextualize the message of Christ into real-life situations.

The unfortunate reality is that this job is becoming more and more difficult as our culture becomes increasingly ungodly. Secular media and humanistic schools of higher education are shaping the way this generation thinks in such a manner as to reject the teachings of Christ as being obsolete and irrelevant. The average young person doesn't even believe in absolute truth or absolute morality. The world has taught us to do whatever feels good. But Christ stepped into the world to remind us that there is a God who is the creator of all men; that He has a specific way He wants all of us to live; and that one day He will come back and judge each man according to His standards and commandments that He has revealed in the Bible.

As Christians, we must fight to keep the teachings of the Bible in the mainstream of our society. We cannot sit back idly and watch as the major influencers of our time seek to remove God from the center of our culture and make Christ a backburner issue at best. We must use all of our God-given creativity, imagination, and charisma to teach people to obey all that Christ commanded us in the Scriptures. Christ's teachings are not bound to any particular period of time, context, or group. Rather, His teachings are timeless, applicable in all contexts, and relevant to all people.

If we are going to fulfill the King's Dream of having Christ-like men and women throughout the world, we must preach to everyone that Christ saves, and we must not be afraid to challenge them to obey all that He has commanded us concerning our lifestyles. By doing this, we are bringing God the most glory, and we are doing the most good for mankind.

Why Should It Matter?

God's dream is to see men become disciples. He loved the Son and wants to see you and me living the way the Son lived and encouraging others to do the same. The dream that drives everything that God does is His dream to see men become like Christ. This dream motivates all of God's decisions. This dream provokes and determines every action of God. This dream is the very reason He sent His only begotten Son. Jesus came and was willing to lay down His life because He loved the Father and wanted His dream to be fulfilled.

Earlier I told you that Satan's worst nightmare is to see you embrace and become excited about God's plan for the world. This is his greatest fear because he knows that if you begin to shape your life around fulfilling God's greatest desire of making disciples, then you will be just as dangerous to him as Peter, Paul, Priscilla, and Aqulia, James and John, and all the rest of those New Testament saints we celebrate for their bravery and faith towards God. What made them so dynamic was their pursuit of God's will with total and reckless abandon. This is why knowing your King's Dream is so important—it is the key that starts the ignition to the motor which drives your life.

Child of God, I want you to know the same joy that I have known. Ever since I made it my goal to pursue my King's Dream, my life has been truly amazing. I have had the joy of preaching the Gospel all over the world, and I have had the privilege of being the pastor for one of the greatest congregations in the country. Most importantly, though, I have seen God use me to transform the lives of men and women daily, as I have challenged them to live their lives for the Master and to become true disciples of Christ. Now, every morning has meaning, and every day is filled with purpose. Though there are challenges and there is opposition, the hope of Jesus Christ so fills my heart that I am convinced that no weapon formed against me shall prosper. And I know the only reason my life has so much passion and power is because I have discovered my King's Dream, which unlocked my Kingdom Dream.

Now that you know your King's Dream, make it your goal in life to discover your unique role within His dream. As you seek to uncover your Kingdom Dream, never lose sight of what God has revealed to be His greatest desire. The following chapters in this book will take you through a five-step process to identifying how you can use your unique God-given talents, skills, creativity, and gifts to turn men into disciples of Christ. By doing this, you will bring maximum glory to God. Remember His promise: if you dedicate your life to being a disciple and making disciples of others, He will be with you always, even unto the end of the age. And the blessing simply of knowing Him might just be the greatest joy of all.

Kingdom Dream Devotional

Devotional Passage

For we are His workmanship, created in Christ Jesus for good works, which God prepared beforehand that we should walk in them (Ephesians 2:10).

Kingdom Question

Who do you believe God has placed in your life to disciple and mentor?

Dream Development Exercise

Write out your testimony and share it with five people over the next week.

6

The Dreamer's Passion
Seek to Know God's Heart!

Ask and it will be given to you; seek and you will find; knock and the door will be opened to you (Matthew 7:7).

As we enter into the next phase of our journey, I hope there is a powerful question roaming through your mind. The question I pray you are wrestling with is, "How do I discover my own personal Kingdom Dream?" Well, over the next few chapters I will attempt to remove all mystery and uncertainty by detailing a practical, Biblical process for discovering God's purpose for your life. At this point, however, let me restate for the purpose of clarity what the Bible declares every Christian's mission in life should be. Simply put, every believer is called by God to "Go and make disciples." This means that you and I are to dedicate ourselves to introducing men and women to Christ and encouraging them not only to confess Him as their Lord and Savior, but also to commit to the process of becoming Christ-like in every area of their lives.

How we go about accomplishing this task is unique to each individual. Our exact approach for winning people to Christ is based upon several varying and deeply personal factors, such as our spiritual gifts, special talents, personality, and mission field. However, the steps to discovering our unique Kingdom Dream are the same for each one of us.

The Bible makes it very clear that if we seek, we shall find. Seeking the right things in life will uncover our destiny and God's will for our lives. The key is to make sure we are seeking what will lead us to God's divine purpose and not just our own carnal dreams. A careful study of the lives of several of the earliest followers of Jesus reveals that there were certain common goals they all sought. These common pursuits led each of them to uncover God's unique purpose for their lives. You see, the key to discovering your Kingdom Dream is seeking the right things. Remember: if you seek, you will find. There are five basic steps in the process of identifying your Kingdom Dream. They are:

Step #1 – Seek to know the heart of God.
Step #2 – Seek to know the Scriptures.
Step #3 – Seek to serve the Body.
Step #4 – Seek to win the lost.
Step #5 – Seek to die to self.

A proper study of history will reveal that, more or less, either formally or informally, this is the approach Kingdom Dreamers have taken throughout time. As a matter of fact, my personal discovery of this five-step process came after intensely studying and analyzing my own journey and that of figures from church history. What I uncovered was a phenomenal similarity of process and approach as it pertains to the discovery and fulfillment of Kingdom Dreams. What was equally amazing was how detrimental removing one or more of the steps in this process was to fulfilling a person's Kingdom Dream.

This is to say that each one of the steps is essential to the overall process. For example, if a person does each step but decides not to seek to serve the body of believers, that person won't be able to successfully fulfill their Kingdom Dream. If a person decides not to seek to die to self, this person, too, would be unable to fulfill their Kingdom Dream. The fact is that each step is necessary and must be taken seriously if you are to discover and fulfill your God-given purpose.

Step #1 – Seek to Know the Heart of God

The Lord told him, "Go to the house of Judas on Straight Street and ask for a man from Tarsus named Saul, for he is praying. In a vision he has seen a man named Ananias come and place his hands on him to restore his sight" (Acts 9:11-12).

Probably, the most impactful Christian the church has ever known was the Apostle Paul. Through the pen and preaching of this one man, the Christian faith exploded upon the world and eventually went on to become the most dominant religion in the world—due to how God used this awesome man. But things did not start off so gloriously for this mighty man of God.

Before becoming the great Apostle, Paul wasn't a follower of Christ, and his name wasn't even Paul. As a matter of fact, he was a persecutor of the saints, and his name was Saul of Tarsus. This name sent chills up the spines of all those who called upon the name of Christ. Saul was a zealous Jew who saw Christianity as an abomination against God, and his goal was to wipe out this new religion by any means necessary.

Saul's carnal dream was interpreted in Acts 9 in what has popularly become known as his Damascus road experience. It was one of the most extreme conversions history has ever recorded. Knocked down from his horse while on his way to torture more Christians, he heard the voice of Christ from Heaven asking him, "Saul, why do you persecute me?" There was nowhere for him to run or hide. He had come face to face with the wrath of God and could not hide the vileness of his heart. But in a great act of compassion, Christ chose not to destroy this evil man, but rather to blind him. This was exactly what prideful Saul needed in order to be humbled and inspired to truly seek the heart of God.

For the first time, Saul had no strength of his own. For the first time, Saul understood that God had a plan for redeeming the world that was far bigger than anything he had been taught up to this point in his life. Immediately, as he recorded in the first chapter of Galatians, he consulted not with flesh and blood, but rather with God. He began to single-mindedly seek the will of the Lord for his life. The Bible declares that for three days straight Saul, who would later become Paul, did nothing but pray. He had come to the place in his life where all he wanted was to know the heart of God. It had become clear to him that he, in his zeal, had wandered far away from what God really wanted for his life, and that he had been persecuting a God he hadn't even known.

It was during this personal quest to know the heart of God that the Lord sent a humble disciple named Ananias to speak to Saul. What the disciple told him must have amazed him, because from that point on, Saul became Paul and sought only to know the Lord. He stopped seeking fame and fortune, popularity and power; instead, he simply wanted to know God. In the purity of this pursuit, he discovered his calling. It was as he cried out to God in prayer night and day; pleading with the Lord that He should show him His face, that Paul was surprised by his purpose.

Just like Saul, before his conversion to Paul, was wrapped up in persecuting saints, many people today are far too wrapped up in having powerful, world-renowned, international ministries. Some are so wrapped up in these large ministries that they never really seek God on a personal level to try to get to know Him and to learn what He wants to do with their lives. Far too many people seek the hand of God for what He gives, instead of seeking the face of God to discover who He is. Far more important to God than you working for Him is you knowing Him.

The first and most important thing to God is your relationship with Him. He wants you to know His heart. In the book of Isaiah, God says that there will come a time when He will write His laws upon the tablets of His people's hearts. This is to say that He will no longer govern His people by external laws but rather internally guide them through loving commandments that will be placed in their hearts as they seek to know Him.

Intimacy Before Ministry

One of the questions that most Christians wrestle with is, "What does God want me to do for Him?" This is a sincere question that must be asked. However, it cannot be our first pursuit. Before we begin to work for God, we need to know who He is and what He loves. The act of getting to know the heart of God is called intimacy, which begins when a person asks three questions of the Lord.

The first question is "Lord, who are you?" Have you ever asked the Lord this question? Have you ever requested that the Lord reveal Himself to you? Many of us have been content knowing facts about the Lord and hearing others preach sermons about their personal experiences with Him. But hearing someone else testify about God will never be the same as knowing Him yourself. Ask yourself this question: do you really know the Lord? Have you ever heard His voice or felt His touch or had Him reveal Himself to you? This may seem a frightening thought, but God doesn't just want you to know about Him; He also wants you to know Him personally. Knowing God personally begins when you ask the Lord the simple question, "Who are you?"

In fact, this is the question He has been waiting for you to ask. This is the question that reveals to Him that you are interested in more than just what He can do for you. This takes your relationship with God from being transactional to being transformational. You see, many Christians treat God like a genie: we feel that He has granted us a certain number of wishes that we must use wisely, so we go to Him only in emergencies or when we desperately want something. But God is not satisfied with this type of transactional relationship. Notice His words in Matthew 7:21-23:

Not everyone who says to me, 'Lord, Lord,' will enter the kingdom of heaven, but only he who does the will of my Father who is in heaven. Many will say to me on that day, 'Lord, Lord, did we not prophesy in your name, and in your name drive out demons and perform many miracles?' Then I will tell them plainly, 'I never knew you. Away from me, you evildoers!'

What a frightening passage of Scripture. The Lord never denied that these people did all of these activities; He simply condemned them for never knowing who He was. They were so busy trying to do works on His behalf that they never stopped to seek to know His heart. Child of God, what you must understand about God is that He sees ministry as activities. And although activities are good, they will never be more important to God than intimacy. As a matter of fact, in God's eyes, in order for any ministry activity to be pleasing, it must be an outflow of intimacy. Intimacy must precede ministry for it to be blessed.

The second question a person should ask when seeking the heart of God is, "What do you love?" When you love someone, you want to know what they love so you can please them. Take me, for example, I knew that I had begun to fall in love with my wife when I asked her what she enjoyed doing and she mentioned home decorating and gardening. I had heard of an upcoming home and garden expo at a local convention center, so I bought tickets for us to go. The truth, though, was that I was not interested in home decorating or gardening in the least.

But I was very interested in her.

I took her to the home and garden expo and found myself enjoying our time together. It wasn't that I had discovered some hidden interest in flowers and gardening. No, I was happy seeing her happy, and I wanted to do what she wanted to do. This was how I knew it was true love.

And this is how our relationship with God should be. We should take pleasure in seeing Him happy. The Bible is full of examples of what makes God happy. He loves it when people forgive one another. He loves it when we help those who are hurting, and He loves it when we make joyful songs to Him. These acts bring great pleasure to the heart of God. In your pursuit to know Him, I encourage you to do a Bible study on the topic of things that please God. It will show you a side of God that you may never have realized existed. Most importantly, when you discover what He loves, try your best to do it!

In the process of discovering what God loves, you will also find out what He hates. Make sure you avoid doing what God hates. You see, one way to define sin is when you and I do the things that God doesn't like. It is really that simple. All we have to do to avoid sin is to not do what breaks God's heart.

I once visited a pastor friend of mine. It was early on in our relationship, and it was the first time I had ever been to his office. We had spent a few minutes talking to one another when he was called out of his office to take care of some business matters. He asked me if he could be excused and walked out of his office, closing the door behind him. When he closed the door, I looked up and saw a quotation that he had typed, framed, and hung on the back of his door. This quotation struck me in the core of my being so much so that I have never forgotten the words that I read that afternoon so many years ago. It said:

"May my heart be broken for the things that break the heart of God!"

In that moment, as I sat alone in that office, I felt like crying. For the first time, I asked myself the question, "Is my heart broken for the things that break the heart of God?" It was as if God took a mirror and pointed it at my cold and callous heart and showed me how truly selfish I had become. I realized then that if I was going to be a great man of God, I was first going to have to seek to know His heart. This has been my quest ever since. I want to know what God loves, and I want to know what He hates. I want my heart to be broken so that His heart might be pleased.

Which leads us to the third question you need to ask God if you are going to have intimacy with Him and know His heart, which is, "How can I please you?" When was the last time you asked God how you could please Him? In today's society, we've been taught that it is God's responsibility to make sure we are happy. We often are guilty of treating God like He is our personal waiter, sent to take our orders and to cater to our wants and whims. But God is Creator, and He is the one who should be served and catered to. I love the King James translation of Isaiah 40:31, which says:

"But they that wait upon the Lord shall renew their strength."

Make it your business to structure your life in such a way that you are free to do any and everything that pleases God. He is drawn to those who truly want to see Him pleased.

Don't Rush the Process!

As you begin to ask God these three questions of intimacy, don't try to move too quickly. Take your time and diligently seek His heart. Remember Hebrews 11:6, which teaches us that God rewards those who diligently seek Him. This means that the process of discovering who He is, what He loves, and how you can please Him may take some time, but it is worth every minute. The act of seeking to know His heart will lay the foundation for your Kingdom Dream, and it will do more than anything else to ensure that you always remain in the center of God's will for your life.

7

The Dreamer's Handbook
Seek to Know the Scriptures!

Thy word have I hid in mine heart, that I might not sin against thee (Psalms 119:11)

Earlier I discussed the threat that selfish ambition poses to your Kingdom Dream. In that discussion, I noted that the key to avoiding selfish ambition is to commit your life to Christ and to involve yourself in the church. However, it is critical that I address the fact that one of the greatest challenges that the church faces in this hour is that many of our leaders have become Christian celebrities, and our pulpits are filled with personalities which are larger than life. The enormous popularity of those who proclaim Christ often ends up drowning out the message of Christ altogether, even for those sincerely seeking to know God's will. In an environment like this, it is easy to find yourself following after a man-made philosophy or organizational agenda instead of the Great Commission Jesus gave to His church.

It's important that you not lose sight of the God-given mission Christ has created for you and fall into an empty pursuit of trying to please prideful, ungodly, secular leaders who are motivated only by what most benefits them. Of course, this is not an attack on the Bible's clear teaching that God has placed men and women into positions of authority to guide His church. Instead, it is simply an acknowledgement of the sad condition that church leadership has fallen into in many segments of the Body of Christ, and of the effect that this may have on your ability to accomplish God's will for your life.

The key to not following the wrong agenda is to know God's Word for yourself. John Wycliffe, the famous translator of the first English Bible, once was quoted as saying:

"My hope is that one day a ploughboy will know the Scriptures just as well as the trained priest."

I, too, share Wycliffe's passion for each and every Christian to know the Scriptures for themselves. The Psalmist David declared that it was his knowledge of and devotion to Scripture that kept him from sinning against God. Put another way, David was able to do that which pleased the Lord because he knew God's Word and kept it in his heart.

This is the next step in your journey to discovering your Kingdom Dream. After you have committed in your heart that you are going to live the rest of your life doing all that you can to please God, then you must begin to passionately study the Bible, because in it alone God has revealed His will. Christians ought to view the Scriptures as a road map that leads us to God. The more frequently we check our road map, the less likely we are to get off the path that God has established for our lives.

Several years ago, my quest to train Christian leaders and lay people to know the Bible led me to direct my church in the establishment of The Detroit Bible Institute. This school provides a one-year pre-seminary diploma in Biblical Studies and, among many other courses, a class on how to study and understand the Bible. Since we opened our doors in 2006, we have been blessed to have several key individuals who, through their priceless contributions, have helped me train hundreds of ministry students in our area. I had the privilege of leading the first Hermeneutics (Bible Interpretation) class in our Institute. It was here where I attempted to lay out the major reasons why it was critical for Christians to properly understand the teachings of the Bible. For your benefit, I will briefly explore each reason.

Christian Belief

A careful study of church history brings to light how seriously the early Christians viewed a proper understanding of God's Word. Convinced that many false teachers would arise, the Apostles urged their followers to be on guard against bad doctrine and to know the teachings of Christ well enough to detect truth from error. This was enormously important because people's beliefs always drive the way they live and ultimately determine their eternal destination. For this reason, the apostles continually warned that teachers should remain true to proclaiming the teachings of Christ, and followers of Christ should search the Scriptures diligently to make sure that they were not being deceived.

Bible knowledge has a very real and practical impact on your ability to live out your Kingdom Dream. A person who misunderstands Scripture will be misdirected and probably will be unable to execute the purpose for which God created them. The Apostle Paul expressed it this way:

But I am afraid that just as Eve was deceived by the serpent's cunning, your minds may somehow be led astray from your sincere and pure devotion to Christ (2 Corinthians 11:3).

Notice that the Apostle Paul explained that the fruit of a correct understanding of Scripture would be a sincere and pure devotion to Christ. We can expect that, if we know the Bible well, the result will be a devotion to Christ cemented in unwavering sincerity and dedication. What Paul was doing was showing the Corinthians that our beliefs about Christ and the faith we have in Him have more than an intellectual effect upon us; they impact our hearts and emotions, as well.

Deception is extremely subtle in most cases, often leaving the deceived unaware that anything has changed within them until it is far too late to avoid devastation. The power of the deception that comes as a result of false beliefs is the fact that it can cause you to think that you are still devoted to Christ while it strips you of your sincerity and purity. As a consequence, many Christians will be serving God having only a form of Godliness, but denying the true power that can only come when one's heart is sincerely and purely devoted to God. Studying God's Word with a desire to know His truth will protect you from being tricked by your own self-will or Satan's subtle deception.

Christian Living

There is no denying that what we believe will determine how we live. One of the most famous passages of Scripture is found in Proverbs 23, in which the writer warns against fellowshipping with and courting the favor of a greedy man. In the King James translation, Proverbs 23:7 states these well-known words: *"For as he thinketh in his heart, so is he."* This little phrase draws a vivid picture for us concerning the impact that our beliefs have upon the way we live our lives. The greatest part of your Kingdom Dream should be seen in every aspect of the way you live. When our lives are marred by sin and unhealthy living, it is normally a sign that we're mistaken in our beliefs about God and His Word.

The Bible gives us many analogies concerning the effect that studying and obeying the Scriptures has upon our lives. One of most memorable is found in the Book of James:

Do not merely listen to the word, and so deceive yourselves. Do what it says. Anyone who listens to the word but does not do what it says is like a man who looks at his face in a mirror and, after looking at himself, goes away and immediately forgets what he looks like. But the man who looks intently into the perfect law that gives freedom, and continues to do this, not forgetting what he has heard, but doing it—he will be blessed in what he does (James 1:22-25).

You should see the act of studying the Scriptures the same way you view looking into a mirror every morning. I rarely leave the house without first checking myself out in the mirror. I do this habitually in order to make sure nothing is out of place and to make sure I don't have any glaring marks or blemishes that will bring me embarrassment. This is precisely what happens when Christians study the Bible. The Word of God will reveal anything that is out of place in your life. It will expose the unhealthy attitudes and emotions you may be harboring. It will force you to evaluate how you interact with others and ultimately will ensure that you look your best on the inside. I do not know of anything that causes me to monitor the way I live my life better than active study and application of the Bible.

Christian Evangelism

Many times, my calling has taken me into some pretty dangerous environments and uncomfortable settings. I have had some amazing opportunities, such as speaking in a mosque where I was surrounded by Muslims and presenting the Gospel in remote villages in Africa where war and rebel attacks were a daily reality. But what drove me to these locations was my conviction that the Bible calls us to take God's Word to those who don't know Him. One such passage is found in Romans:

> *... for, everyone who calls on the name of the Lord will be saved. How, then, can they call on the one they have not believed in? And how can they believe in the one of whom they have not heard? And how can they hear without someone preaching to them? And how can they preach unless they are sent? As it is written, "How beautiful are the feet of those who bring good news!"* (Romans 10:13-15).

I am convinced that Christians who do not study the Bible will not evangelize the world. As I have stressed throughout this book, evangelism must be at the core of every Kingdom Dream. If it is not, our pursuits are only carnal activities that in the end will be fruitless. God's great passion is to see people saved. His desire is that none should perish but that all should have everlasting life. This is the message that we will be constantly confronted with each time we open the Bible and study God's Word. Both the Old and New Testaments are accounts of the great lengths to which God was willing to extend Himself in order to redeem and heal lost humanity.

Bible study, if done correctly, should revive our thirst to see lost souls saved. This is one of the major reasons I urge my students to revisit the Scriptures over and over as they seek to live out their Kingdom Dream. I am not only convinced that a proper understanding of God's Word will fan the flame of our evangelistic fervor; I am also persuaded that the Bible is the only tool able to liberate the hearts of men. In other words, our witnessing will lack power if we are not presenting people with the truth found about Jesus in the verses of the Bible.

God wants to use you as a powerful instrument of His glory, but the depth to which your service to Him will be determined is by your commitment to knowing and living out His Word. The more you know of the Scriptures, the greater effectiveness you will have as you reach others for Christ. You will be astonished by how radically transformed the individuals God allows you to touch will be when you present them with the truth found in God's Word. I encourage you to make the study of Scripture your daily discipline.

Christian Community

There are two influences which God intends to work together in order to keep His church united. The first is the abiding presence of the Holy Spirit in our lives.

The very act of baptism symbolizes our immersion into the Body of Christ by the Holy Spirit. The Holy Spirit lives in each true believer and works to bring us into perfect unity with one another. The second agent of unity among Christians is the Word of God. Since the Bible acts as the final authority on faith and practice among Christians, our adherence to its commands testifies to our salvation and brings us into oneness with other believers.

Our oneness is tremendously vital to the mission of Christ being accomplished. This message is clearly seen throughout the Gospel of John. What John intentionally and strategically records are the teachings of Jesus that seem most to stress the need for our unity and agreement. This can best be seen in John 17:20-23:

> *My prayer is not for them alone. I pray also for those who will believe in me through their message, that all of them may be one, Father, just as you are in me and I am in you. May they also be in us so that the world may believe that you have sent me. I have given them the glory that you gave me, that they may be one as we are one: I in them and you in me. May they be brought to complete unity to let the world know that you sent me and have loved them even as you have loved me.*

Notice several key observations within the text.

The first is that it would be the Apostles' message that would unite us. Jesus proclaims here that our submission to that message was going to unify us into a community of believers whom the world would be able to recognize as His followers. The second key observation found in the text is that our oneness would provide credibility to Jesus' claims that He had been sent by God to save the world.

What an awesome thought to consider that without our unity, the world would lack the needed evidence for believing that Jesus was truly the Christ and sent by God the Father to be the savior of the world. But how would this unity be experienced? The answer is that unity will only come when Christians seek to know the Scriptures and have a proper understanding and adherence to the Word of God

My hope is that, through more examination of each of the reasons that Christians should study their Bible and seek to know the Scriptures, you have come to realize that without a strong Biblical foundation, your Kingdom Dream will lack both power and direction. Every Christian should do their best to be trained to their maximum potential on how to study Scripture and live out God's Word. Your Kingdom Dream requires far more than just inspiration if it is going to have the potency needed to impact the world. As you seek to know the Scriptures, expect God to transform both your mind and your heart.

✛

Kingdom Dream Devotional

Devotional Passage

All Scripture is given by inspiration of God, and is profitable for doctrine, for reproof, for correction, for instruction in righteousness, that the man of God may be complete, thoroughly equipped for every good work (2 Timothy 3:16-17).

Kingdom Question

What is the best time in my daily schedule for me to study the Bible and who can I ask to hold me accountable to my daily Bible study time?

Dream Development Exercise

Purchase a one-year bible and commit to reading through the Bible in a year.

8

The Dreamer's Service
Seek to Serve the Body of Christ

The kingdom of God does not come with your careful observation… (Luke 17:20)

O ne field of study that has always fascinated me is sociology, the study of human societies and cultures. What I find to be most intriguing about this science are the findings and insights sociologists give us about the way particular groups of people think and behave. Although I am not a sociologist, I believe that all evangelists and pastors should be keen students of culture if they plan to effectively reach people for Christ.

As someone who has had the privilege of growing up in America and spending time in both Europe and Africa in my adult years, I have observed a very interesting common trait among individuals who are a part of this generation. It seems that we, especially in the West, are totally obsessed with success. Everyone wants to achieve great status, fame, and fortune. This may not sound terribly surprising or seem to be unique to this period of time in human history. True enough, people through the ages and in every culture have wanted to win, be victorious, and accomplish great things. However, I believe technology has produced an impatience that has added a new impediment in the quest for success: the need for speed. Many feel they shouldn't have to take the long road to victory or slowly build a reputation. Instead, we want success and we want it now! Television shows like *American Idol* and *Who Wants to be a Millionaire?* have become cultural icons and have fed our frenzied delusions of overnight stardom.

The problem with this irrational thirst for immediate results is that it creates within most of us a love affair with the end product and a hatred for the developmental process. Everyone loves the diamond with all its shimmering beauty, but no one is interested in the countless hours of digging and sifting through the dirt that it took to discover that picturesque jewel. We all celebrate the graduation, but few get excited about the grueling tasks of study, homework, and research that it takes to make the grade. What Scripture reveals about this is that God is just as concerned with the process as He is with the end product.

Many of us are type-A personalities, competitive, highly driven overachievers who want it now and want it perfect. For us, the thought of having to go through a long process of labor and character development makes no sense and seems to be a waste of precious time. If we are not careful, we will allow this flawed way of thinking to have a hugely negative impact upon our Kingdom Dream. Kingdom Dreams take time to develop. God is not interested in making you an overnight success; He would much rather you be built to last. Why does it take time for Kingdom Dreams to develop? Because it takes time for Kingdom Dreamers to develop.

One of the primary methods that God uses to develop His Kingdom Dreamers is to have us labor in our local churches for long seasons of preparation before He unleashes us on the rest of the world. Often, these seasons of servitude are marked by very little recognition and many challenging assignments meant to wage war against our egos. Once we have been sufficiently humbled, God will usually reveal Himself in unforgettable ways, testifying to His faithfulness and glory in our lives. We see this very clearly in the life of Moses. After Moses had served faithfully on the back side of the desert without any applause, awards, or recognition, God finally spoke to Moses from a burning bush, declaring to him, *"I am with you"* (Exodus 3:12).

Not everyone will have a burning bush experience, but we must all serve in our local churches. The next step in your journey to discovering your Kingdom Dream is for you to begin to seek to serve the Body of Christ. Those who skip or ignore this step usually end up doing more harm than good to God's people and His plan. But for those who are willing to submit themselves to the authority of their local church and serve the Body in meekness and faithfulness, God will use them mightily to bless the lives of many.

God is interested in testing you in some critical areas during this time of serving in your local church. A test has two primary goals. First, a test is designed to confirm your areas of strength; and second, a test reveals your areas of weakness. Once you have been strengthened in the weak aspects of your life, God will then entrust you with the opportunity to do your unique assignment.

One common mistake we all make whenever God shows us His purpose for our lives is to assume that His desire is for us to begin doing that specialized purpose right away. However, this typically is not the case. As a matter of fact, the Bible is full of some very prominent examples of great individuals who had long periods of waiting and serving between the times when God revealed His ultimate will for their lives and His releasing them into their calling. Such figures as Moses, whom I previously mentioned, served 40 years before God released him to be the leader of Israel. King David served 16 years under Saul before he was ordained King. Joseph labored in obscurity for 17 years before he was introduced as Prime Minister of Egypt. The list goes on and on, and if you are faithful, one day your name will be added to the list of faithful servants of God who didn't despise or skip this step in the process.

Principals of Serving

There are several principals you must embrace if you are going to effectively complete this phase of your Kingdom Dream discovery process. The first is that God wants us to serve in general capacities before He allows us the joy of fulfilling our specific assignment. This is a difficult principal for many of us to accept, primarily because it requires great levels of humility and patience. If this is frustrating, simply trust that your Kingdom Dream will come to pass, and remind yourself every day that God is as interested in the process as He is in the end product.

The second principal you must embrace during your seasons of serving is that God is looking for trustworthy people, not talented people. Many of us believe that God has called us because we are gifted or intelligent or highly skilled, but the fact is that God has not selected you for any of these reasons. God can select whomever He wants, however He wants, whenever He wants; He is most interested in individuals He can trust. The Apostle Paul famously communicates this principal in this statement found in 1 Corinthians 4:2 (KJV):

Moreover it is required in stewards, that a man be found faithful.

God wants to know if He can trust you before He promotes you. He is looking to see if, in both small and large tasks, you can be trusted. He wants to see if, in both good and bad times, you can be trusted. He wants to see if, in both easy and difficult times, you can be trusted. Once you have proven your trustworthiness, then and only then can you be released to live the Kingdom Dream God has created for you to live.

The Three Questions of Trust

I am a long way away from where it all began for me. In many ways, I am sometimes still amazed at the fact that I am a pastor at a phenomenal and growing church, overseeing a Bible Institute, and reaching tens of thousands of lives daily through Equipped for Life Media Ministries. The reason it's so astonishing to me is that I know where I came from. After God first spoke to me and revealed His calling for my life, I shared it with my pastor. I didn't know what to expect, but I knew I was anticipating something related to preaching and teaching. Much to my surprise, his first ministry development assignment for me was to clean up the youth room after every church service. He handed me a broom and showed me where the waste baskets were and congratulated me on my call into the ministry. For the next several years, I came in early and stayed late after church to make sure the youth room was free from wadded-up paper, debris, and bubble gum stuck under the chairs. I became acquainted with the vacuum cleaner, and I made it my job to make sure every seat in the small gathering area had a Bible placed on it.

That time was vital to my development. Although the job wasn't glamorous or deeply spiritual on the surface, I realize now that God was asking some very important questions of me during those days. The first question He was asking was, "Can I trust you to do what you don't want to do?" I have to admit it was somewhat humbling and embarrassing to tell people that God had called me to preach, when in fact I'd only officially been called to clean the youth room. Gratefully, I was mature enough to recognize what God was trying to develop within me and, to this day, I am glad I took the assignment seriously and cleaned that youth room to the best of my ability.

Unfortunately, most of us fail this test and never graduate to the next step. Rarely are people willing to do what they don't like to do. If, by chance, some of us do submit to the authorities in our lives and accept the unwanted assignments, we often do it with reluctance or a bad attitude, or both. The fact is, if we can't prove to God that we can be trusted to do what we don't want to do, He will never be able to release us to serve Him in greater ways. Once we prove ourselves, more tests come—the farther you go in your calling, the fewer freedoms you have to do only what you want to do and the more He will call on you to do things you don't want to do.

This is clearly seen in the case of Jesus' road to Calvary. Although Jesus wanted to see every man saved, He was not looking forward to what He knew He had to endure: being mocked, beaten, and separated from the Father. But His commitment to us and to the Father drove Him to be faithful even when He didn't want to be. We see this in Matthew's Gospel where he records:

> *Going a little farther, he fell with his face to the ground and prayed, 'My Father, if it is possible, may this cup be taken from me. Yet not as I will, but as you will'* (Matthew 26:39).

Jesus realized that if He was to be the Messiah of the world, He would have to be willing to pay a high price: crucifixion. His great desire for our salvation dictated that He would have to take our sins upon Himself and endure the agony of the Father's wrath and judgment. But thank God He did it, both because of the salvation it secured and because of the example He set for you and me to follow.

The second question God seeks to challenge us with during our times of serving in general capacities is "Can I trust you to serve those whom you don't want to serve?" Probably the most popular parable of Jesus is the story of the Good Samaritan. Many of us appreciate what this story represents about how we should care for others who are hurt or in need. However, few of us truly understand the historical context of this story. During the time of Jesus, the hatred between Samaritans and Jews was severe. Jews looked down on Samaritans for their mixed heritage and theological heresies. This dislike often led Jews to disrespect, mistreat, and belittle the Samaritan people. For a Samaritan to help a suffering Jew would be the modern day equivalent to a black person helping a hurting member of the Ku Klux Klan or a Jewish person helping a radical Islamic extremist who despises his existence. Why did Jesus use this when teaching His followers? Because He wanted to challenge their thinking on what it meant to serve God.

Matthew 5:43-45 tells us:

You have heard that it was said, 'Love your neighbor and hate your enemy.' But I tell you: 'Love your enemies and pray for those who persecute you, that you may be sons of your Father in heaven. He causes his sun to rise on the evil and the good, and sends rain on the righteous and the unrighteous.'

This is one of the traits that distinguishes a follower of Christ from the rest of the world. We are not simply called by God to love and serve those we have a natural affection for, but we also have to demonstrate our ability to love those we find no connection or resonance with. Don't be surprised if, during this step in your process of discovering your Kingdom Dream, God has you working with difficult people, serving under harsh leaders, or ministering to ungrateful individuals. All of this is simply God's way of asking you, "Can I trust you to serve those whom you don't want to serve?"

During this tough time, we must remember what it truly means to be a follower of Jesus. Notice who the Bible declares Jesus died for: He died on behalf of sinners, even the ones who rejected His love, broke His commandments, and nailed Him to a cross. These were the ones to whom Jesus was referring when He cried out, *"Father, forgive them, for they do not know what they are doing*" (Luke 23:34). Before God will allow you to walk in the fullness of your Kingdom Dream, you must first answer the question "Can He trust you to serve those whom you don't want to serve?"

The final question God asked me in those early days—which He will surely ask of you, also—is, "Can I trust you to be faithful when you don't want to be faithful?" Have you ever been discouraged by all the unfaithful people around you? Have you ever wanted to stay home and not show up to an assignment just so others can see how it feels to be stood up or disappointed? I've wrestled with these kinds of thoughts plenty of times. There are times when we all get tired both physically and emotionally. It is during these moments when it is most tempting for us to simply not show up for a task that God has called us to do, especially if the task might seem like a small one.

I caution you: beware of moments of weariness when everything in you is telling you to be unfaithful. In these instances, our internal warfare causes many of us to fall short; in these instances, it must seem to God like we cannot be trusted. That's why you must force yourself to be faithful to God—even in the small things, and even when you don't want to be faithful. You see, God knows we will never accomplish His great calling for our lives if we are unfaithful. Time and time again in those early days of the development of my ministry, I was asked to show up for events that seemed uninteresting to me; to tackle tasks that seemed unappealing; and to work with unfriendly people. Although my track record wasn't perfect, I did try my best to show up when asked, with a good attitude and a grateful spirit. I don't know how to measure the impact my faithfulness in those moments assists me now, but I know it was vitally important then because I was answering God's question, "Can I trust you to be faithful when you do not want to be?" with a resounding "yes."

Ultimately, God is calling you to serve the Body of Christ in small, difficult, and often humbling ways, because He is trying to develop you into a trustworthy person. He wants you to mature to the point that He can entrust to your care His most prized possession—His precious people. Don't plan on getting to the summit overnight or to have immediate stardom as a minister of the Gospel. Plan to be called to the unseen places by God to do the undesirable assignments that no one else wants to do. If you are faithful, He will reward you with your Kingdom Dreams. So the next time a church leader asks you to serve, no matter what the assignment, look deep into your heart and repeat the words of Isaiah:

Here am I. Send me! (Isaiah 6:8)

Kingdom Dream Devotional

Devotional Passage

Read 1 Corinthians, Chapters 12 through 14

Kingdom Question

When have you had the greatest joy while serving others?

Dream Development Exercise

Meet with your pastor or a member of your church's leadership team and ask them how you can best serve within your local church.

9

The Dreamer's Pursuit
Seek to Win the Lost

The fruit of the righteous is a tree of life, and he who wins souls is wise (Proverbs 11:30).

By now, I am sure you have gathered that at the very heart of every Kingdom Dream should be a passion to see the unsaved come to know Christ. I have intentionally tried to be somewhat repetitive concerning this theme. The reason for my redundancy is not a forgetful mind, but rather a sensitive spirit to the primary message of Scripture. If the Bible is about anything else, it is surely about God's desire to save and redeem those lost in sin.

Earlier I mentioned that many segments of the Body of Christ are in trouble because, for long periods of time, they have majored in the minor doctrines of the Bible and minored in the major teachings of Scripture. This has produced a sort of upside-down church in which the needs of the individual are emphasized and exalted above God's. The focus of preaching and worship became an attempt to make sure that the worshipper was having an enjoyable experience, instead of making sure God was being honored by our reverence.

We have taken God from the center of our devotion and replaced Him with images and idols of ourselves.

This is why very few Christians ever come to fully realize God's call—the call of God is a call to selflessness and personal denial, which isn't a popular philosophy. It is, however, the one philosophy that needs to be proclaimed to today's generation if there is any hope for the Kingdom of God to advance.

However, even after we have mentally ascended to the place where we are able to embrace the Christ-centered life, we must fight to maintain this conviction amid all of the opposing messages constantly bombarding us. That is where witnessing and evangelism play a big role. Soul-winning is central to helping us maintain our focus on bringing God glory with our lives.

The next step in the journey to discovering your Kingdom Dream is to seek to win souls. In a recent telephone conversation, my brother told me that he had reached the stage where he was ready to begin sharing his faith with others. His zeal was clearly evident, even over the phone, and his emotions stirred my heart as we spoke. But despite his enthusiasm, he also expressed the need for some practical tips for someone like him who was just beginning to actively share his faith in Christ with others. Naturally, I was deeply moved and overjoyed by his request.

Much of what I will share in this chapter will be for individuals just like my brother who aren't advanced or experienced evangelists. I will try my best not to assume that you have been trained on the basics of witnessing, and I pray that this chapter will be inspiring and informative in your pursuit of your Kingdom Dream and God's glory.

Why Is Evangelism So Important?

It's hard to get excited about something we can't see the value in. For years, this was true for me concerning evangelism. I had heard sermons on the topic and knew that as a good Christian I was supposed to actively share my faith with others, but I couldn't see much of a direct benefit. I simply assumed those who really wanted Christ knew where He was and could go to the church whenever they were ready. I also assumed that anyone who had a different worldview than mine had the right to think their own way. After all—who was I to impose my convictions on another person? About eight years ago, that all began to change.

There wasn't one specific experience or sermon that I could point to that created in me a passion for sharing my faith; rather, there was a mounting sense in my spirit that there was more to being a Christian than going to Sunday service and midweek Bible study. Then, one day I ran across a verse of Scripture that gripped my heart in a way I'd never expected. The verse was Proverbs 14:28:

A large population is a king's glory, but without subjects a prince is ruined.

On the surface, this verse may not seem to be speaking about much at all to most people. But for me, during that season of my life, it spoke volumes. What I heard God saying so loudly and urgently was that His glory increases with every new addition to His Kingdom. This meant that if I were truly going to do all I could to bring God glory, I had to base my plans on introducing non-Christians to Christ. Evangelism was no longer merely a discipline to undertake so I could feel good about myself; rather, it became a joyous act done from a heart, which desired to bring God glory.

Once I came to understand that the primary value of witnessing was that I was adding to the glory of God, I wanted to share my faith with as many people as possible. For the first time, I began to see how much God loves sinners. I finally realized that Jesus' death on the cross was to demonstrate His love for all the people of the world, both good and bad. It was this revelation, combined with my genuine desire to show the love of Christ to others, that became the motivation for sharing my faith. For the Christian, the height of human love is seen in our willingness to witness to others in an authentic hope for their salvation.

The benefits of sharing our faith are many. We benefit greatly any time we discuss our faith in Christ with others, especially with those who have never been offered the invitation to make Christ the Lord of their lives. It is hard to accurately express the ways my life has been transformed as a result of me witnessing to my family, friends, and loved ones, and to total strangers, as well. However, there are three specific benefits you'll receive once you start witnessing.

The first benefit you'll get from sharing your faith with non-believers is that your heart will be kept pure. This is because our natural tendency is to focus on our own needs and wants, but evangelism, if done sincerely, drives you to pray for the needs of others. Once you begin to build relationships with people who don't know Christ, you will find yourself seeking the Lord on their behalf, petitioning God for their salvation. There currently are three individuals in my life I'm desperately petitioning God to save. My heart wants for them to know the security and joy that I have as a Christian. We should want this for others; it is a pure desire. The more we share our faith, the more this desire grows;

and the more this desire grows, the more purity grows in our lives.

The second benefit to witnessing is that it keeps our focus right. Jesus warns us to not build up treasures on earth. This acts as a reminder to us all that our focus has to be on eternity instead of on the temporary affairs of life. Witnessing reminds us that our time on earth is brief, but that eternity is forever. Several years ago, this thought led me to create an acronym for our church in order to keep us focused on God's call for us to be His witnesses. I use the word S.H.A.R.E., which stands for:

> *Sacrificing to*
> *Help*
> *Another*
> *Reach*
> *Eternity*

As a pastor, I know that if my church is going to be and remain healthy, we must not lose our focus on fulfilling the Great Commission and introducing people to Christ. Sharing our faith is essential to maintaining our focus to see God glorified through us. Any time you stop witnessing, you will begin to drift away from God's call for your life, and you will probably lose passion for your Kingdom Dream as well.

The final benefit that you will see when you begin to actively share your faith is that witnessing will keep your mind sharp. I spend many hours on a weekly basis studying my Bible and learning all I can about my faith. Part of the reason for this is that I am constantly being confronted with questions and challenges to Christianity when I am witnessing. Many people have concerns and misunderstandings about what Christians profess to believe, so it is our job to make sure we address these concerns and answer the questions the world is asking. Witnessing forces you to become a better student of your faith in order to be able to answer any questions or objections you encounter.

I share this with you, not to frighten you, but because most people truly are looking for a savior and will be forever grateful when you share Christ with them. However, it's important to be prepared for difficult encounters. People need us to have answers to their questions, because if we don't, they will assume that there are no answers to the questions they are asking. I encourage you to read books on how to defend your faith, on church history, and on what Christians believe. Being sharp and informed will allow you to win souls to God and bring Him maximum glory.

How Do I Share My Faith with Others?

Evangelism can be terribly intimidating. The thought of having to talk to people about your religious beliefs can, for some, be disconcerting and awkward.

For most of us, this is true because no one has ever really taught us how to share our faith in a way in which it becomes a joy. We all know we should be talking to others about Christ, but we usually don't know how to get the conversation going or how to bring someone to commitment. With this in mind, I want to give you four steps to sharing your faith in such a way that you will become a natural witness of Christ to others.

First, share your fellowship with them. In other words, you should first seek to build genuine relationships with non-Christians. Most Christians don't actively seek relationships with non-Christians. This is often because we don't want to be tempted by their behavior to live in ungodliness. But look at Jesus' example. Jesus told His disciples He didn't come for the well but for the sick. He was criticized for spending much of His time with irreligious people, but His goal was to show them His sincere interest in who they were as people.

This is vital to effective witnessing. If people think they are merely our assignment, they will see straight through our religious talk and won't be moved by our theology. When, on the other hand, people are convinced that you honestly want what's best for their lives, they will listen long and earnestly to what you have to say about Jesus.

Although many methods of evangelism have become popular in the church, such as passing out tracts and witnessing on street corners, the most effective way to reach people for Christ is to share your faith with them in the context of a true and real relationship. Remember that the purpose of the relationship is to bring them to Christ, and not simply to hang out together. I encourage you to begin your evangelism with those you already know and love. These individuals have seen your lifestyle up close and will be open to your invitation to become a Christian.

The second step to effective witnessing is for you to share your testimony with others. What is a testimony? Our testimony is simply the story of our lives told in three parts. The first part is the time before we met Christ. It is important that you share who you were prior to Christ so others can relate to you. Far too often, Christians only communicate our successes, leaving non-Christians to feel that we are out of touch with reality and can't really relate to their problems and issues. When non-Christians are able to hear about your struggles with sin, immorality, depression, or emptiness, they are able to identify with you as a person. However, I caution you to not be too explicit about your past when sharing with others. We should focus our conversations on those facts and details that are important to leading them to Christ, and not inadvertently brag about our wild days before Christ.

The second part of your life story should be the details of how you came to know Christ. This is when you can share with them how someone loved you enough to confront you with the truths of the Gospel and to challenge you to evaluate the direction of your life. This will allow them to have a deeper understanding of why you feel compelled to share your faith with others. You want to be sure to let them know what it was like when you finally knew that you were saved. Share with them the emotions you experienced at the time of your conversion.

The third part of your life story should be the season of your life since you have become a Christian. It is okay to let them know of the ups and downs life has brought you since you invited Christ to come in, but be sure to convey the peace you have in knowing that He is with you and that Heaven is your home. Testify to them of the joy of being a Christian and the awesome purpose and meaning your life now has since you decided to follow Christ. You will be amazed at how many people will stop you and express to you that they would like to have the joy and peace that is clearly evident in your life.

The next step to sharing your faith with others is to share with them the truth about the consequences of rejecting Christ. This is often the most difficult aspect of any conversation concerning becoming a Christian. By nature, we all want to focus on the positive aspects of becoming a believer, but the Scriptures also reveal that those who reject Christ suffer on earth and throughout eternity. Hell is a real place. Those of us who believe in Heaven and God must also believe in Satan and hell, because the same Bible testifies to all four. It is important that we try not to placate those who seem to be resisting God's offer of salvation. The price is far too great for them to ignore God's grace. There will be some who will not seriously consider accepting Christ until they are confronted with the painful cost of their decision.

Finally, if you are going to effectively share your faith with others, you must be willing to patiently share your love with all. Love never fails; it conquerors all. Our love is what will penetrate the hearts of those to whom we witness. Our love will speak louder to them than our theology or our debates. Actively pray and ask God to fill your heart with compassion for all those you come into contact with. Do your best to be gentle and gracious, even with the hardest of non-Christians. Practice doing random acts of kindness as a way of showing them the love of Christ. Above all, care enough for their eternal destinies to overcome your fears and tell them about Jesus.

Kingdom Dream Devotional

Devotional Passage

The Parable of the Great Supper

Now when one of those who sat at the table with Him heard these things, he said to Him, "Blessed is he who shall eat bread in the kingdom of God!"

Then He said to him, "A certain man gave a great supper and invited many, and sent his servant at supper time to say to those who were invited, 'Come, for all things are now ready.' But they all with one accord began to make excuses. The first said to him, 'I have bought a piece of ground, and I must go and see it. I ask you to have me excused.' And another said, 'I have bought five yoke of oxen, and I am going to test them. I ask you to have me excused.' Still another said, 'I have married a wife, and therefore I cannot come.' So that servant came and reported these things to his master. Then the master of the house, being angry, said to his servant, 'Go out quickly into the streets and lanes of the city, and bring in here the poor and the maimed and the lame and the blind.' And the servant said, 'Master, it is done as you commanded, and still there is room.' Then the master said to the servant, 'Go out into the highways and hedges, and compel them to come in, that my house may be filled. For I say to you that none of those men who were invited shall taste my supper' (Luke 14:15-24).

Kingdom Question

Who do I know that is passionate about sharing their faith?

Dream Development Exercise

Create a prayer list of 12 people in your personal life who don't know Christ.

10

The Dreamer's Surrender
Seek to Die to Self

Then he said to them all: "If anyone would come after me, he must deny himself and take up his cross daily and follow me" (Luke 9:23).

Congratulations! You have arrived at the final step in the journey to discovering your Kingdom Dream. By now I pray that you have made commitments to seek God's heart, seek to know the Scriptures, seek to serve the Body of Christ, and seek to win the lost. As I stated previously, the key to finding your Kingdom Dream is to seek the right things. No doubt, if you have already begun to seek after God in these areas, the Lord has already begun to speak to your heart concerning His will for your life. I hope your imagination is racing as you consider the awesome ways you can use your life as an instrument for God's glory. Don't be surprised if you are beginning to find it difficult to focus on certain pursuits that, at one time, used to dominate your mind and attention. This simply means your heart is being consumed with a new passion. This new passion is from God, and what has awakened within you is the very mission for which you were created to fulfill.

You may have noticed, though, that your Kingdom Dream journey grows progressively less inspirational and more challenging the farther you go into it. This is because the farther we go into God's plan for our lives, the more He reveals the cost we must be willing to pay for His glory. Though your salvation is free, your Kingdom Dream will cost you everything. In many amazing ways, however, the more you give up for God, the more He gives to you. Truly, Jesus is right when He tells us that if we lay down our life for Him, we will find everlasting life in Him.

It rightfully could be said, then, that fulfilling your Kingdom Dream will be the toughest job you will ever love. The imagery presented to us in the words of Jesus recorded in Luke's Gospel is not designed to provoke feelings of pleasure or thoughts of comfort. These piercing words strike to the core of our cozy, well-planned lifestyles, jarring us into a new reality. Jesus is unapologetic in the bluntness of His recruitment message. He tells us flatly, and with a loving yet brutal honesty, that the price for following Him is total self-denial.

And, ultimately, a cross.

In our culture, crosses have become nice, polished symbols of a faith that have successfully assimilated into mainstream culture. The fact is, however, that crosses were not always this safe and unthreatening. The cross that Jesus embraced on our behalf was not finely hued or smoothed to a glossy finish, nor was it perfectly stained and burnished to appear to be appealing. Rather, it was a rugged symbol of a painful death. I am acutely aware of the fact that the very word "death" is unattractive and dissuasive when you are attempting to inspire someone to abandon their comfortable life of ease in pursuit of God's glory. However, a cross is the only picture Jesus provides for what it means to be a true follower of Christ. To be a Kingdom Dreamer is, in many ways, to be a cultural martyr. It is to say, "I reject the societal pressures to be shallow, superficial, and self-centered." To be a Kingdom Dreamer is to be a non-conformist to dead religion and lifeless church activities that have no eternal value and produce no disciples for Christ. This, my friend, is the unveiled truth that Jesus has been praying for you and me to embrace; this is the cost of bringing Him glory with your life. This is the pathway to your Kingdom Dream.

This final step in the journey is for you to seek to die to self. All polite words have been exhausted to this point; what is left is the frank and sometimes abrasive charge of a Savior who knows full well what He is requesting of His followers. Jesus never lowers the bar or lessens the prerequisites for walking with Him. He still says boldly to you and me, "Let the dead bury the dead, but you come and follow me!" With emphatic conviction, He reminds us that nothing we give up for the Kingdom's sake will be of great worth, and that what we will receive in return for trusting Him with our future will be of everlasting value. You will be blessed beyond measure in ways expected and unexpected, externally and internally, seen and unseen. Most of all, if you are willing to die to self, you will have the supreme joy of knowing Him.

Fortunately, for many of us—especially Christians in America—the death we must die is very rarely physical. It is more often a death to our wants, agendas, and preferences. It is a death to safe and risk-free living. It is a death to the control we think we have over our own lives. Let's examine four areas of loss you will experience in exchange for the great joy of knowing and fulfilling your Kingdom Dream.

The Loss of Control

The Apostle Paul famously penned in Galatians 2:20 that he had been crucified with Christ, that he no longer lived, and that Christ now lived through him. These are the words of a man who had matured to the point of finally realizing that he was no longer in charge of his own life, but that it was Christ's loving and protecting hands that had taken over. God had been ordering Paul's footsteps ever since the moment he submitted his life to Christ and committed to chasing after his Kingdom Dream. The result was not just the salvation of many, but God had taken a man who declared himself to be the chief of all sinners and transformed him into a beautiful testament of the love and power of Christ. God was now showing Paul off to the world as a beaming treasure in the crown of the Master.

This all happened because Paul resisted the fear to turn total control of his life over to the Lord. We are used to managing our own affairs. We are most at ease when we are in charge of our own choices and dictating our own direction. Many of us have bought wholeheartedly into the philosophy that says, "This is my life, and I can do with it whatever I please!" However, this way of living is not what God requires of the Kingdom Dreamer. We must turn over our hearts, relinquish our right to decide, and submit our wills to His command if we are going to fully please Him. This by no means suggests that we no longer have the obligation to think or are somehow relieved of our responsibility to make decisions, but it does insinuate that we must never forget whose children we are and who is in charge over us.

The wonderful actuality of not being in control of our own lives is that the one who is in control is duty-bound to provide for whatever He chooses. This is a pledge that God is more than willing to make and, more importantly, to keep. He promises that:

> ... *everyone who has left houses or brothers or sisters or father or mother or children or fields for my sake will receive a hundred times as much and will inherit eternal life* (Matthew 19:29).

Your allegiance to Christ will dictate the forfeiture of your own dominion over your life, but it will also produce a glorious freedom. This freedom comes from knowing that servants and children of God are guaranteed the promise of the full provision required to meet all of their needs. This means that you will never be without anything essential in your life. Your cup will run over as you see His mercies renewed day by day on your behalf. This blessing and peace comes only when we are willing to release total influence over our lives unto God.

The Loss of Carnality

To be carnal means to live sinfully, to do that which

displeases God, or to follow fleshly desires. The consistent teaching of the New Testament concerning the lifestyles of believers is the doctrine of holiness. The Apostles tell their audience repeatedly that if we are to please God, we must live spiritually pure and morally righteous lives. To be spiritual or holy doesn't mean that you won't come into contact with the world, nor does it imply total perfection from moral failure. But it does communicate a deep commitment on our part to do that which is right in the eyes of God, on a continual basis. The Apostle Paul put it this way:

The mind of sinful man is death, but the mind controlled by the Spirit is life and peace; the sinful mind is hostile to God. It does not submit to God's law, nor can it do so. Those controlled by the sinful nature cannot please God (Romans 8:6-8).

As a Kingdom Dreamer, you must redefine concepts like pleasure, fun, and entertainment. These words can't continue to mean what they meant before you came to know Christ or committed to pursuing your Kingdom Dream. Again, I know this is difficult because it will represent the discontinuation of certain activities and relationships that are spiritually unhealthy for you as you seek to fulfill your calling. However, don't be misled into thinking that righteous living is somehow boring or not enjoyable. The greatest pleasures of my life have come as a result of following God. My closest friendships and most entertaining activities no longer have the residue of guilt and remorse attached to them. Now, I can spend a whole evening at an event and leave feeling excited, edified, and closer to God. This is a benefit that comes into our lives only when we are willing to sacrifice our own carnality. As one person humorously said concerning his new life in Christ, "I didn't stop dancing; I just changed partners."

I encourage you to evaluate your life and identify any activity or relationship you may be involved in that discourages you spiritually. Once the Holy Spirit has shown you where you need to make changes, begin to pray and ask God to renew your mind and replace your desire for the unhealthy with the desire for the healthy.

Our Kingdom Dreams can easily be subverted by carnal ways of thinking and behaving. As Paul stated, the carnal mind can't receive anything from the Lord. This means that any time we are living carnally, we have essentially disconnected ourselves from God's influence and direction in our lives. Long seasons of carnality will inevitably lead to self-destruction and the loss of our Kingdom Dream, so do your best to live your life according to the Word of God and with the goal of pleasing Christ in all you do.

The Loss of Comfort

As I am writing this book, the 2008 Olympics are in progress. Athletes from all around the world have been waiting four years for these two intense weeks of competition, all with the same hope of bringing home gold. Sometimes I think about the training regimen that these world-class competitors must endure to be the best at their particular sport. The hours of running and lifting weights; the practices day after day; the waking up before dawn to get an edge on your opponent; the eating restrictions; the mind-numbing repetition; the injuries—none of this is easy or comfortable. Then again, what makes champions is giving up one's right to be comfortable. You can't be comfortable and set a world record in track and field. You can't be comfortable and compete on the highest levels of gymnastics, and you can't be comfortable and beat the reigning champion in your sport. If you are going to achieve at the highest level, you must be willing to give up your comforts.

I don't know where your Kingdom Dream will take you or what it will fully demand of you, but I do know that if you are going to bring God the maximum glory, you must be willing to do what no one else is willing to do. If you are going to transform this world on Christ's behalf, you must be willing to go where no one else wants to go. If you are going to win the gold, you can't take it easy or be laid back or live a relaxed life; these are luxuries only losers can afford. I know that doesn't sound too friendly, but the Scriptures command us thusly:

> *Do you not know that in a race all the runners run, but only one gets the prize? Run in such a way as to get the prize. Everyone who competes in the games goes into strict training. They do it to get a crown that will not last; but we do it to get a crown that will last forever* (1 Corinthians 9:24, 25).

Paul urges us to consider the great lengths to which athletes are willing to go in order to claim a prize that is temporary and has no eternal value. His challenge to us is to adjust our perspective on what it means to be a Christian. His premise is simply that if those who gain what is only valuable for a moment deny themselves certain comforts for the sake of victory, we must be willing to die daily for our King to be glorified.

I have come to realize that no external comfort I sacrifice for God, such as giving up certain recreational activities or giving away major portions of my income to help advance the Gospel, can compare with the great internal comfort I have in knowing that God is with me and is well pleased with who I am.

Take heart in the fact that the greatest promise in the Bible is Jesus' declaration in Hebrews 13:5 that, *"Never will I leave you; never will I forsake you."* Understand, though, that the journey to fulfilling your Kingdom Dream will not be an easy one. It will require greater surrender at every turn, and, just when you feel you have given all you can give, God gently whispers to you, *"My grace is sufficient for you."* Take heart in knowing that He will never ask of you more that you are able to give and never demand that you endure more than you can bear, but He will call you to deny yourself, take up your cross, and follow Him daily.

This is the death that we all must die if our Kingdom Dreams are going to take hold. We must be willing to lose our control, lose our carnality and, most of all, lose our comforts for His sake. For the rare and chosen few who are willing to pay this price, the rewards are immeasurable. Through you, lives will be changed, captives will be set free, the hopeless will be given hope, the world will be transformed, and, most importantly, Christ will be glorified.

Kingdom Dream Devotional

Devotional Passage

Therefore we also, since we are surrounded by so great a cloud of witnesses, let us lay aside every weight, and the sin which so easily ensnares us, and let us run with endurance the race that is set before us, looking unto Jesus, the author and finisher of our faith, who for the joy that was set before Him endured the cross, despising the shame, and has sat down at the right hand of the throne of God (Hebrews 12:1-2).

Kingdom Question

To whom do you believe that God has called you to submit to?

Dream Development Exercise

Pray and ask God whom He would have to disciple/mentor you. Then ask this person if they would be willing to hold you accountable and help you grow?

11

Protecting Your Kingdom Dream

Finally, be strong in the Lord and in his mighty power. Put on the full armor of God so that you can take your stand against the devil's schemes (Ephesians 6: 10-11).

In many ways, discovering your Kingdom Dream is similar to giving birth. Like a woman in labor, you are now pregnant with a vision that has the potential to change the world. With this awesome privilege come tremendous responsibilities. The greatest responsibility you now have is the duty to protect your Kingdom Dream with all the diligence and might you possess.

The battle to maintain your focus may be the toughest obstacle you now face. There will be unrelenting forces coming against you each and every day, tempting you to abandon your calling and revert back to the life of comfort you enjoyed prior to accepting your calling to bring God glory. The cancer of comfortable Christianity will try its best to infect your mind and contaminate your thinking concerning God's will for your life.

Over the course of my ministry, I have helped many people travel the road to discovering their Kingdom Dream. Some dropped out of the process early on, while others made significant progress toward their destiny but ultimately refused to pay the price for that which God had called them to do. A few, though, through sheer resolve, have been blessed to discover their God-given purpose. But even those did not all see their Kingdom Dream survive. The reason for this spiritual collapse in the lives of so many sincere Christians is not a lack of desire, but rather a lack of training in the art of spiritual warfare. Never forget that you and I will have to fight to maintain possession of everything that the Lord, through His grace, has delivered unto us.

As a boy growing up in Detroit, it was imperative that I knew how to fight and defend myself. In Detroit, the weak don't survive and the soft are crushed by the harshness of city life. I was blessed to have an uncle who realized that knowledge of basic self-defense skills was necessary if I were going to make it in my neighborhood, so he took it upon himself daily to teach me how to form a fist, block an attack, and throw a punch. He also taught me the psychology of fighting. I can still hear his words echoing in my mind now: "Never look scared, Chris"; and "Always look your opponents in the eyes"; and "Never start a fight, but if someone starts one with you, be ready to finish it." These were just some of the survival strategies he instilled into his young nephew, all because he wanted me to make it and to have an advantage over my enemies.

Likewise, I want you to make it; that is why I have designed this entire chapter to do for you spiritually what my uncle did for me physically. I want to teach you how to fight. Training is spiritual warfare, and it should be required for all Christians who dare make the commitment to honor God with their lives. The church cannot continue to send out unprepared troops into the world. I have promised to do all I can to make sure you are not just another casualty.

The first step in spiritual warfare is to do reconnaissance. This is a military term that refers to the act of gathering information about your enemy so you can know their methods of and motives for fighting. Knowledge of our enemy is absolutely vital if we are to have any hopes of fulfilling our Kingdom Dream. There are three enemies you must be aware of:

The Devil

To say that Satan is going to do all he can to attack and undermine your efforts to fulfill your destiny is an understatement. You should expect nothing less than all-out war. Your enemy doesn't fight fair, nor does he relent. His animosity toward you finds its basis in his eternal hatred and contempt for God and everything the Lord has ordained. Since God's hand of grace is upon your life, the devil has aligned himself against you and has determined to resist you with all his strength. The Apostle Peter warns:

> *Be self-controlled and alert. Your enemy the devil prowls around like a roaring lion looking for someone to devour* (1 Peter 5:8).

Very few Christians have an accurate understanding of who Satan truly is and how he operates. Most of us think of Satan in one of two ways. Either we marginalize him and think of him in only practical terms, imagining of him as a cartoon character instead of a real being, failing to recognize the spiritual realm that exists beyond our physical selves; or we deify him, overestimating his power and influence. Let me attempt to provide you, then, with a balanced and realistic view of Satan.

Firstly, it is important to establish that Satan is not God. This means that Satan is not all-powerful, all-knowing, or all-present. Christians should not have a dualistic worldview that sees the universe as being governed by two equal and oppositional forces, one good and one bad. No, God has no equal. Satan only exists because the Lord saw fit to allow him to remain in order to fulfill the greater purpose of human redemption.

Of course, we should never take our enemy lightly. Satan is not a weakling or a pushover. He is a spiritual terrorist who possesses an artillery of weapons of mass destruction. He has studied human behavior for thousands of years and has formed a strategy to ruin the lives of God's men and women that has worked very well for him over the course of history.

Although Satan is not all-powerful, he does have great powers of deception. The Bible, in fact, says his deception will be so strong in the end times that if God had not shortened the days, even the very elect would be deceived. We must realize that although Satan is not all-knowing, he is fully aware, often more than we are, of what God is doing. He knows the Word of God and is very subtle and crafty in his distortion of Scripture, preying upon our ignorance and lack of diligent study. Finally, we must embrace the fact that, although he is not omnipresent, he has an army of demons that consists of a third of the fallen angels of Heaven, all of whom he has strategically positioned throughout the world in order to make it seem as if he is everywhere.

The most crucial fact that you must understand

about Satan, though, is that he can be defeated. The Bible acts as a handbook of spiritual warfare. Satan will not be able to conquer the Christian who studies the Bible exhaustively and applies its teachings consistently. If we live according to the Word, then God's presence will be with us, and Satan will not have a chance. The devil knows that he has no hope of overpowering you as long as you are walking closely with God, so he will send people and opportunities your way in an attempt to lure you away from God. Your primary defense is to walk in the Spirit and maintain your intimacy with the Lord.

The World System

Our society is not designed to promote spiritual maturity or obedience to God. Western culture, for the most part, has been contaminated by the ungodly and aggressively spreads the insidious philosophies of Satan. We live in a fallen world. That is why we must expect to be inundated with messages of lust, greed, selfishness, and corruption. These ideas we find in the form of humor, marketing, and everyday speech. They are so pervasive that they feel as natural to us as water does to a fish. But the blessing in being a Christian is that God has awakened our spirits to the madness of the world and the foolishness of ungodly living. Still, we must be continually on guard.

The primary tool used by the world system in order to pervert us from God's original design for our lives is the media. Movies, television shows, music, video games, and marketing campaigns all carry with them very powerful messages that are often hard to detect and usually anti-Christian in nature. Many Christians regularly and happily expose themselves to forms of media that blatantly deny Christ and His teachings under the guise of entertainment. The average person in our society sees more than 10,000 sexual images a year on television. Drug use, adultery, and violence are treated so lightly in this environment that most of us become numb to their potential to devastate our lives. If we don't stand up against this type of bombardment, we have no hope of winning in our battle to bring God glory.

Our hope for defeating the attacks upon our conscience that come through the media is to set righteous and godly standards. You should not permit yourself to watch every movie that comes into your local theatre; indulge in every form of entertainment that airs on your television; or respond to the pressure put upon you by creative marketers to live your life in a way that seems appealing to the masses. If you resist the temptation of the world to poison yourself with its media, you will have more than a fighting chance of fulfilling your Kingdom Dream.

Of course, I am not recommending that you cut off all contact with the world and live the life of a monk. What I am saying is to be careful not to work against yourself and to recognize that your mind is easily influenced to follow the suggestions to which it is exposed. Make sure what you watch and listen to is edifying and uplifting to your spirit. If something is causing you to act or think carnally, turn it off and protect yourself from its sway over your life. Remember the words of the Apostle Paul when he said to the Roman Christians that:

> *Everyone has heard about your obedience, so I am full of joy over you; but I want you to be wise about what is good, and innocent about what is evil* (Romans 16:19).

The Flesh

The final enemy you must fight is your sinful nature, which consists of all of the rebellious thoughts and desires that dwell inside of you. The Book of Galatians speaks of the war constantly raging within each one of us. Paul told the Christians in Galatia that:

> *...the sinful nature desires what is contrary to the Spirit, and the Spirit what is contrary to the sinful nature. They are in conflict with each other, so that you do not do what you want* (Galatians 5:17).

Paul wanted his followers to know that, although they had been born again, they still possessed a sinful nature that had to be brought under subjection. We cannot ignore that, for many of us, our worst enemy is the man in the mirror. The great comedian Flip Wilson had a famous saying whenever he messed up: "The devil made me do it!" I believe that Christians blame far too much on the devil.

The primary way that our sinful nature wars against us is through our thoughts. Often we are driven by fleshly desires, which may be temporarily pleasing physically, but are an open act of rebellion against God and a spiritually destructive indulgence. We have to know that the problem of wickedness and evil in the world is not simply external. Scripture declares that:

For out of the heart come evil thoughts, murder, adultery, sexual immorality, theft, false testimony, slander (Matthew 15:19).

For most of us, the sad reality is that we have been sabotaging the very blessings that God, in response to our prayers, has sent into our lives. So how do we defeat ourselves without destroying that which is good and pleasing to the Lord? The answer is to monitor our thoughts carefully. Philippians 4:8 provides us with the following instruction:

Finally, brothers, whatever is true, whatever is noble, whatever is right, whatever is pure, whatever is lovely, whatever is admirable—if anything is excellent or praiseworthy—think about such things.

This means that you have the right to reject any thought which is inconsistent with the Word and with the will of God for your life. You also have the power to intentionally think upon topics and concepts that are true, excellent, spiritual, and praiseworthy, as well as those that are part of your Kingdom Dream. Exercise your authority—be the doorkeeper to your mind and don't allow every thought admission into your heart.

As you can see, this requires 24-hour vigilance. The harsh reality is that you are not allowed to take vacations from your job of governing your thoughts. We are in a war, and war demands total dedication and unwavering focus. God has equipped you with every weapon you will need to maintain healthy, Christ-centered thinking. You must use your weapons against any way of thinking that does not conform to the teachings of the Bible. In his letter to the Corinthians, the Apostle Paul advised:

For the weapons of our warfare are not carnal, but mighty through God to the pulling down of strong holds; Casting down imaginations, and every high thing that exalteth itself against the knowledge of God, and bringing into captivity every thought to the obedience of Christ (2 Corinthians 10:4-5).

If you are willing to diligently police your thoughts and filter out those which are not from God, then you will undoubtedly achieve all that God has purposed for your life. The flesh is a powerful foe, but it can be defeated. By God's grace and through continual evaluation, you can have the mind of Christ.

Final Tips for Protecting Your Kingdom Dream

I thank God for you, and I want you to know that I have committed myself to praying for you daily. My hope is that God's great and magnificent purpose for your life will come to pass, and that He will use you mightily as an instrument of His glory. I know the road will not be easy, but let me remind you that it is worth it. The blessings of living for Christ are more wonderful than words can express. So do your best to honor Him every day of your life. Live with your eyes toward eternity and your heart toward God. Above all, never forget your Kingdom Dream is what He created you for; accomplish it on His behalf, and, as you do, give all the glory to the Lord.

There are four activities I'd like to suggest you commit yourself to for the rest of your life. These activities have helped me immensely in my quest to fulfill my Kingdom Dream. I pray they will be a blessing to you as well.

1. Celebrate God's goodness daily.

2. Connect with other Kingdom Dreamers regularly.

3. Call upon your advisors frequently.

4. Communicate with God continually.

Thank you for taking the time to learn to discover your Kingdom Dream and for letting me be your coach. Your journey has just begun, and, by God's grace, I am persuaded that the best is yet to come for your life. Let the dream begin!

Kingdom Dream Devotional

Devotional Passage

Read Galatians Chapter 5

Kingdom Question

Which *Fruit of The Spirit* are strongest in your life and which Fruit are weakest?

Dream Development Exercise

Write out your Kingdom Dream and give it to a prayer partner, your discipler and pastor.

About the Author

Christopher W. Brooks has been enthusiastically involved in ministry for nearly twenty years. In that time, he has ministered to thousands through pastoring, speaking at workshops and conferences, as well as through the ministry of Equipped for Life Media. With its outlets in television, Internet and international radio broadcasts, Pastor Brooks has touched the lives of millions with his encouraging, yet challenging messages that bring to life the pure Word and Power of the Gospel.

Pastor Brooks is the Senior Pastor of Evangel Ministries, a thriving 1500-member church in the heart of Detroit. With the mission of evangelizing the world, he and his dynamic team have created and implemented numerous programs, curriculum and outreaches that "Equip Christians, Enrich Families and Empower Communities." He is also the president of the Detroit Bible Institute, which is committed to raising up the next generation of Christian leaders who will impact their world for Christ.

A graduate of Michigan State University with a B.A. in Finance, Pastor Brooks is also a graduate of the Oxford Centre for Christian Apologetics at Oxford University, and is currently pursuing a M.A. in Christian Apologetics at Biola University. He and his wife Yodit are the proud parents of Christopher and Zewditu and live near Detroit, Michigan.

To contact Pastor Brooks, call, write, or e-mail us:

Equipped For Life
P. O. Box 39258
Detroit, MI 48239
(313) 836-7732

www.equippedforlife.tv

To order additional copies of *Kingdom Dreaming* or to find out more about life-changing resources whose mission is to glorify God, expand His Kingdom and change the world through the power of the written and spoken word, please visit Zoe Life Industries' website www.zoelifepub.com or Pastor Brooks' website www.equippedforlife.tv.

You can also contact Zoë Life Publishing at:

Zoë Life Publishing
P.O. Box 871066
Canton, MI 48187
(877) 841-3400
outreach@zoelifepub.com